THE NINETEENTH-CENTURY SENSATION NOVEL

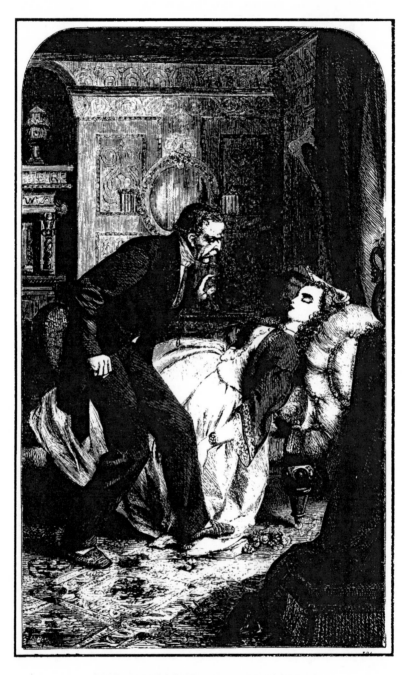

'DREAMING LOVE AND WAKING DUTY'

by Robert Barnes arws 1840–1895 from *London Society* 1862, Vol. 2

W

THE
NINETEENTH-CENTURY
SENSATION NOVEL

Lyn Pykett

Second Edition

NORTHCOTE
BRITISH
COUNCIL

© Copyright 1994 and 2011 by Lyn Pykett

First published in 1994 by Northcote House Publishers Ltd, Horndon, Tavistock, Devon, PL19 9NQ, United Kingdom.
Tel: +44 (0) 1822 810066 Fax: +44 (0) 1822 810034.

Revised and expanded second edition 2011

British Library Cataloguing-in-Publication Data
A catalogue record for this book is available from the British Library

ISBN 978 0 7463 1212 4

Typeset by PDQ Typesetting, Newcastle-under-Lyme
Printed and bound in the United Kingdom

Contents

Note on the Expanded and Updated Edition

The earlier version of this book, which first appeared in 1994 as *The Sensation Novel from The Woman in White to The Moonstone*, charted the re-emergence into critical view of a nineteenth-century fictional genre which had, in its own day, enjoyed immense popular success and generated heated critical and moral debates. Since the mid-1990s the sensation novel has continued to attract the attention of both general readers and critics and scholars. In the last fifteen years the sensation novel has been brought to fresh audiences in numerous new editions and in new television, radio, film and stage adaptations. There have also been numerous new critical studies of the novels of Wilkie Collins, Mary Elizabeth Braddon and Ellen Wood, as well as an attempt to shift attention from an exclusive focus on these authors and a relatively narrow range of sensation novels published in the 1860s. *The Nineteenth-Century Sensation Novel* responds to these developments, taking account of recent studies of sensation fiction, and expanding both the range of authors covered and its discussion of the authors originally included.

Abbreviations and References

Wherever possible quotations from sensation novels are taken from widely available paperback editions, or a modern library edition as follows:

A   Wilkie Collins, *Armadale*, ed. Catherine Peters (Oxford: Oxford University Press, 1999).

AF   M. E. Braddon, *Aurora Floyd*, ed. P.D. Edwards (Oxford: Oxford University Press, 1999).

B   Wilkie Collins, *Basil*, ed. Dorothy Goldman (Oxford: Oxford University Press, 1990).

CUF   Rhoda Broughton, *Cometh Up As A Flower*, ed. Pamela Gilbert (Peterborough, Ontario: Broadview Press, 2010).

DW   M. E. Braddon, *The Doctor's Wife*, ed. Lyn Pykett (Oxford: Oxford University Press, 1998).

EL   Ellen Wood, *East Lynne*, ed. Elisabeth Jay (Oxford: Oxford University Press, 2004).

H&S   Wilkie Collins, *Hide and Seek*, ed. Catherine Peters (Oxford: Oxford University Press, 1999).

JML   M. E. Braddon, *John Marchmont's Legacy*, eds. Toru Sasaki and Norman Page (Oxford: Oxford University Press, 1999).

LAS   M. E. Braddon, *Lady Audley's Secret*, ed. David Skilton (Oxford: Oxford University Press, 1998).

L&L   Wilkie Collins, *The Law and the Lady*, ed. Jenny Bourne Taylor (Oxford: Oxford University Press, 1999).

LC   Florence Marryat, *Love's Conflict*, ed. Andrew Maunder, *Varieties of Women's Sensation Fiction, 1855–1890* (London: Pickering and Chatto, 2004), vol.2.

M   Wilkie Collins, *The Moonstone*, ed. John Sutherland (Oxford: Oxford University Press, 1999).

NN   Wilkie Collins, *No Name*, ed. Virginia Blain (Oxford: Oxford University Press, 1998).

SME   Ellen Wood, *St Martin's Eve*, ed. Lyn Pykett, *Varieties of Women's Sensation Fiction, 1855–1890* (London: Pickering and Chatto, 2004), vol. 3.

WW   Wilkie Collins, *The Woman in White*, ed. John Sutherland (Oxford: Oxford University Press, 1996).

1

The Sensation Phenomenon

WHAT WAS SENSATIONAL ABOUT THE SENSATION NOVEL?

Sensation became the rage and sensations were demanded every hour.[1]

In 1863, in the pages of the *Quarterly Review* (a heavyweight organ of conservative opinion) Henry Mansel, then Waynflete Professor of Metaphysical Philosophy at Oxford and later Dean of St Paul's, launched a fierce critical and moral attack on a species of fiction which was just then enjoying considerable success. The literary phenomenon about which Mansel wrote – in both sorrow and anger – was the sensation novel, which, he claimed: 'must be recognised as a great fact in the literature of the day, and a fact whose significance is by no means of an agreeable kind'.[2] Nearly one hundred and twenty years later Patrick Brantlinger described the sensation novel as 'a minor subgenre of British fiction that flourished in the 1860s only to die out a decade or two later'.[3]

A 'great fact' in the literature of its day? A 'disagreeable' sign of its times? An ephemeral, minor subgenre? What was the sensation novel? Why did it come to dominate the literary scene for a time in the 1860s? What did it signify? What, if anything, does it have to offer to twenty-first-century readers of novels, students of fiction and students of Victorian culture? These are some of the questions which this book seeks to address.

The 1860s was a decade of sensational events and sensational writing. It was the age of '"sensational" advertisements, products, journals, crimes, and scandals',[4] and of sensational 'poetry, art, auction sales, sport, popular science, diplomacy and

1

preaching'.[5] The 1860s was also, pre-eminently, the age of the sensational theatre, most notably the stylized dramatic tableaux, heightened emotions and extraordinary incidents of melodrama. As Michael Booth has so amply demonstrated, in *Victorian Spectacular Theatre, 1850–1910* (1981), this was an age of increasingly spectacular 'special effects', involving dioramas, panoramas, elaborate lighting systems and machinery of all kinds. Theatrical illusion and Victorian machine culture combined in a new technology of representation. In short, this decade was a moment of consolidation in the 'era of the spectacle' – inaugurated by the French Revolution, and consolidated by the Great Exhibition of 1851 and the International Exhibition of 1862 – in which the 'mode of amplification and excess' became 'a mode of producing the *material* world'.[6]

Private affairs were turned into public spectacle in the theatre of the courtroom. A novel form of real-life drama drew the salaciously inclined to the newly constituted divorce courts (following the Matrimonial Causes Act of 1857) to hear details of marital deception, discord and misalliance. Bigamy cases were another source of such courtroom dramas. Between 1853 and 1867 some 884 cases of bigamy were heard in the English courts and 110 in Scotland. In 1861 the newspapers were full of details of the colourful and convoluted Yelverton bigamy case in which Maria Theresa Longworth sought to invalidate the marriage of Major Charles Yelverton to a Mrs Forbes by proving that she herself was the Major's lawful wife. This long-running legal wrangle, which became a kind of newspaper serial, highlighted the chaotic state of the marriage laws and marriage customs in England, Ireland and Scotland and also provided sensation novelists with many incidents for their plots.[7]

The criminal courts also threw the spotlight on to 'the secret theatre of home'[8] with a number of sensational trials for crimes of passion and tales of domestic violence in the late 1850s and early 1860s. Murderous women were especially in the news, most notoriously Madeline Smith, who poisoned her lover by putting arsenic in his cocoa (1857), and Constance Kent the sweet 16-year-old who was accused of stabbing her 4-year-old brother in the famous Road murder case in 1860.[9] The details of all of these cases of bigamy, divorce and murder were communicated to the ever-widening readership of a rapidly expanding newspaper press by the sensational reporting then enjoying a vogue.[10] Sensational journalism (like sensation fiction) was seen by many as a form of creeping contagion, the means by which the world of the common streets, and the violent or subversive deeds of criminals were carried across the domestic threshold to violate the sanctuary of home.

The sensation novel was among the chief sensations of this sensational decade. According to some contemporary reviewers and commentators on the literary scene the sensation novel was a mushroom growth, a new kind of fiction which appeared from nowhere to satisfy the cravings of an eager and expanding reading public possessed of suspect, or downright depraved tastes. 'Two or three years ago', observed a writer in the *Edinburgh Review* in 1864:

> nobody would have known what was meant by a sensation novel; yet now the term has already passed through the stage of jocular use...[and is] adopted as the regular commercial name for a particular product of industry for which there is just now a brisk demand.[11]

In one of many of the examples of 'jocular use' found in *Punch* – a parodic prospectus for an invented journal called *The Sensation Times* – the sensation 'product' was described as:

> devoted to Harrowing the Mind, making the Flesh Creep...Giving Shocks to the Nervous System, Destroying Conventional Moralities, and generally Unfitting the Public for the Prosaic Avocations of Life'.[12]

Throughout the 1860s and into the 1870s 'sensation' or 'sensational' were ubiquitous critical or descriptive terms. During this period, as Philip Edwards has noted, 'almost every novel reviewed was either sensational, or remarkable for not being so'.[13] Writing in 1867, Margaret Oliphant noted that 'all our minor novelists, almost without exception, are of the school called Sensational'.[14] Wilkie Collins, Mary Elizabeth Braddon, Ellen (Mrs Henry) Wood and Rhoda Broughton were indisputably sensation authors in the 1860s, although their long careers stretched well beyond the sensation boom and often took them into different fictional territory. Sheridan Le Fanu and 'Ouida' (Marie Louise de la Ramée) were sometimes reviewed as sensationalists. However, Le Fanu rejected the label, claiming (in his Preface to his novel *Uncle Silas*) to belong to the 'legitimate school of tragic English romance', and Ouida's exotic novels of racy high life might perhaps be seen as belonging to the genre of high society romance. Charles Reade used sensation techniques, particularly those borrowed from the domestic melodrama of the theatre (for which he also wrote), but he preferred the term 'matter-of fact-romance' for his often sensationalized novels with a social purpose. Charles Dickens, whose *Great Expectations* was reviewed alongside Collins's *The Woman in White*, undoubtedly shared many of the sensationalists' subjects and methods, and was sometimes included among their number. Trollope and George Eliot escaped the label, but, as I shall show in a later section, did not escape the thing. Thomas Hardy made a notable late contribution to the genre with *Desperate Remedies* (published in 1871 but written in 1869) which he dismissed, rather too lightly I think, as a 'highly conventional and sensational tale'. In the first edition of this book (published in 1994) I followed Kathleen Tillotson and Philip Edwards in regarding Collins, Braddon and Wood as the main exponents of the genre, and focused more or less exclusively on their work in the 1860s. These three writers and the 1860s retain their central position in this revised edition, but I also respond to the upsurge of work on the sensation novel in the last two decades, which has expanded our ideas about the sensation novel in interesting ways, by looking beyond what Andrew Maunder has described as 'this "A" list trio',[15] and by looking both backwards and forwards from the 1860s.

Variously described as 'fast novels', 'crime novels', 'bigamy novels' or 'adultery novels', sensation novels were pre-eminently tales of modern life. As a reviewer in the *Quarterly* put it:

> The sensation novel, be it mere trash or something worse, is usually a tale of our own times. Proximity is, indeed, one great element of sensation. It is necessary to be near a mine to be blown up by its explosion; and a tale which aims at electrifying the nerves of the reader is never thoroughly effective unless the scene be laid in our own days and among the people we are in the habit of meeting.[16]

These electrifying novels of 'our own days' were mainly distinguished by their devious, dangerous and, in some cases, deranged heroes and (more especially) heroines, and their complicated plots of secrecy, mystery, suspense, crime and horror. The sensation plot usually consisted of varying proportions and combinations of duplicity, deception, disguise, the persecution and/or seduction of a young woman, intrigue, jealousy, and adultery. The sensation novel drew on a range of crimes, from illegal incarceration (usually of a young woman), fraud, forgery (often of a will), blackmail and bigamy, to murder or attempted murder. Formally sensation fiction was less a genre than a generic hybrid. The typical sensation novel was a catholic mixture of modes and forms, combining realism and melodrama, the journalistic and the fantastic, the domestic and the romantic or exotic. Like stage melodrama, with which it had so much in common, the sensation novel was, as Dickens wrote of Wilkie Collins's *The Moonstone,* 'wild yet domestic'.[17]

What were the common characteristics of the narrative structures in which these melodramatic plots were articulated? Thomas Hardy named four key aspects of the sensation narrative in his description in the Preface to the 1889 edition of his own attempt at the genre (*Desperate Remedies*): 'Mystery, entanglement, surprise and moral obliquity'. Entanglement and surprise are, of course, commonly found in the heavily plotted Victorian novel, but the sensation narrative is more than usually reliant on surprising events and extraordinary coincidences for its effects, and character is quite often subordinated to incident and plot. Mystery too is a staple ingredient of the mainstream Victorian novel, but in the sensation novel it is the dominant element. The sensation novel, like the detective novel, is the quintessential novel-with-a-secret. The moral obliquity noted by Hardy is just one of the consequences of the sensation narrative's obsession with secrecy. The narrative satisfactions of the sensation novel depend to a great extent on the gradual uncovering of the central secret(s). To this end the most effective sensation writers developed techniques of narrative concealment and delay or deferral. Collins, for example, developed the split or shared narrative which used a variety of first-person narrators, none of whom was in possession of the whole story. Braddon and Wood have recourse to a kind of narratorial coyness, declining (sometimes explicitly, at others implicitly) to disclose crucial items of information, or having key events occur off-stage (so to speak) and only revealing their occurrence at the denouement. Sensation novelists in general, but particularly Collins and Braddon who were closely involved with the theatre, developed a dramatic narrative method, and made a great deal of use of set-piece scenes and dramatic tableaux. Whatever the technique adopted the result was the same: a modification, in some cases quite radical, of the omniscient narrator's role as the reader's guide, guardian and friend. Without this helping hand, and in the absence of all the facts of the case, the reader is left to make provisional moral judgements as the narrative unfolds. The result is a considerable degree of moral ambiguity.

These thrilling novels caused a sensation with both readers and reviewers. Several sensation novels – notably Wilkie Collins's *The Woman in White*, Mary Elizabeth Braddon's *Lady Audley's Secret*, and Mrs Henry Wood's *East Lynne* – were numbered among the best selling novels of the nineteenth century. The sensation novel's spectacular success with readers in the 1860s, and the apparent tendency for sensation topics and techniques to invade all areas of contemporary fiction, made the sensation fiction phenomenon one of the hot topics of discussion for the Victorian 'chattering classes'. In an anonymously published review of 'Sensational Novelists' for *Blackwood's* in 1862, Margaret Oliphant linked the emergence of literary sensationalism to wider cultural and political trends, not least the waning of that mid-Victorian optimism about a new age of peace and prosperity which had found its expression in the Great Exhibition of 1851. 'Ten years ago', Oliphant wrote:

> the age was lost in self-admiration...We were about to inaugurate the reign of universal peace...we had invented everything that was most unlikely, and had nothing to do but to go on perfecting our inventions...What a wonderful difference in ten years! We who once...declared ourselves masters of all things, have relapsed into the natural size of humanity before the great events which have given a new character to the age.

In Oliphant's view, whether one liked it or not, it was entirely unsurprising 'in an age which has turned out to be one of events' – such as the Crimean War and the American Civil War – that art and literature should 'attempt a kindred depth of effect and shock of incident'.[18] More specifically, Oliphant linked the rise of sensationalism in the novel to a reaction against the fashion for 'domestic histories' which 'however virtuous and charming' lacked – in Oliphant's view – a compelling narrative. Other reviewers were impressed by the boldness of the subject matter, the skilful plotting and innovative narrative techniques of the sensation novel. However, many commentators on contemporary life and letters saw sensation fiction as both cause and symptom of the depravity of contemporary morality and the modern sensibility. The existence of the genre was taken to be evidence of a cultural disease, and its success was described as an epidemic comparable with the 'Dancing Mania and Lycanthropy of the Middle Ages'; like these diseases 'the Sensational Mania in literature burst[s] out... in times of mental poverty, and afflict[s] only the most poverty-stricken minds'.[19] In short, the sensation novel was held to be yet further evidence of that emotional and spiritual degeneracy of modern urban-industrial culture against which Wordsworth had fulminated in his Preface to *Lyrical Ballads* in 1800, when he noted that: 'a multitude of causes, unknown to former times, are now acting with a combined force to blunt the discriminating powers of the mind, and... reduce it to a state of almost savage torpor'. Chief among these causes was 'the encreasing accumulation of men in cities, where the, uniformity of their occupations produces a craving for extraordinary incident, which the rapid communication of intelligence hourly gratifies'. The 'literature and theatrical exhibitions of the country', where 'frantic novels' and 'sickly and stupid German tragedies' prevailed in place of the works of Shakespeare and Milton. In the 1860s Wordsworth's condemnation of the modern 'craving for extraordinary incident' was echoed by Henry Mansel, who consigned the sensation genre to 'the morbid phenomenon of literature – indications of a wide-spread corruption, of which they are in part both the effect and cause'.[20]

Mansel, like other reviewers (some of whom were following his lead), also wrote disapprovingly of the way in which sensation fiction appealed to the reader's physical appetites, and of its penchant for 'preaching to the nerves'. Mansel suggested that reading sensation fiction produced a bodily rather than a cerebral response, that, as Alison Winter puts it, 'the route from page to nerve was direct',[21] and that the only way to distinguish between these novels is by reference to the

7

kind of sensation which they aim to produce: '[t]here are novels of the warming pan, and others of the galvanic battery type – some which gently stimulate a particular feeling, and others which carry the whole nervous system by steam'.[22] The seductive and potentially corrupting appeal of what the *Christian Remembrancer* described as the sensation novel's power of 'drugging thought and reason...[and] stimulating the attention through the lower and animal instincts'[23] was a preoccupation of many reviewers in the 1860s and 1870s. Sensation novels were often described as either opiates or stimulants which overpowered or suppressed rational thought and morality, and heightened nervous responsiveness. There was also widespread concern about the sensation novel's undue influence on impressionable readers – particularly the young and women – which had its origin in mid-Victorian assumptions about gender and in particular in 'suppositions about women's affective susceptibility'.[24] As well as being seen as an unhealthy form with an unhealthy influence, the sensation novel was also thought to have an unhealthy interest in madness. According to one contemporary reviewer, this preoccupation with madness enabled sensation authors to stretch probability or dispense with it entirely and offered them a way of transcending the limitations of a prosaic and materialistic age.[25]

One of the most shocking and thrilling aspects of sensation fiction, as far as its first readers and reviewers were concerned, was the fact that the action of these fast novels of crime and passion usually occurred in the otherwise prosaic, everyday, domestic setting of a modern middle-class or aristocratic English household. In fact both modernity and domesticity are more than simply the *mis-en-scène* of the sensation novel, they are also among its main preoccupations; they are topics of discussion and investigation. In the sensation novel the matter and manner of the Gothic tale, the crime novel and domestic fiction meet and mingle in a modern English setting in which 'the England of today's newspapers crops up at every step'.[26] Sensation novels, as Henry James wrote in a much-quoted review of M. E. Braddon's *Aurora Floyd*, dealt with:

> those most mysterious of mysteries, the mysteries which are at our own doors...Instead of the terrors of Udolpho, we [are] treated to

the terrors of the cheerful country house, or the London lodgings. And there is no doubt that these were infinitely the more terrible.[27]

Another notably shocking feature of the genre was the centrality of female characters and the way in which women and the feminine were represented. E. S. Dallas's comments in *The Gay Science* (1866) serve as an elegant summary of all those critics who felt that sensation fiction's representation of women breached both aesthetic and social decorum as well as breaking with nature. Dallas refers to the novelist as 'he', but his comments are of the kind that were also – perhaps even more frequently – made on women writers:

> The first object of the novelist is to get personages in whom we can be interested; the next is to put them in action. But when women are the chief characters, how are you to set them in motion? The life of women cannot well be described as a life of action. When women are thus put forward to lead the action of a plot, they must be urged into a false position. To get vigorous action they are described as rushing into crime and doing masculine deeds... the novelist finds that to make an effect he has to give up his heroine to bigamy, to murder, to child-bearing by stealth in the Tyrol, and all sorts of adventures which can only signify her fall. The very prominence of the position which women occupy in recent fiction leads by a natural process to their appearing in a light which is not good. This is what is called sensation. It is not wrong to make a sensation; but if the novelist depends for his sensation upon the action of a woman, the chances are that he will attain his end by unnatural means.[28]

Certainly, one of the most distinctive features of sensation fiction was the way in which it displayed women and made a spectacle of femininity, whether of the passive, angelic, victimized variety (such as Isabel Vane in *East Lynne* or Laura Fairlie in *The Woman in White*) or in the form of the *femme fatale* (Braddon's Lady Audley or Lydia Gwilt in *Armadale*). Whether she is the heroine or the villainess (and sometimes the distinction between these two roles is fascinatingly blurred), at least one of the female protagonists in a sensation novel is likely to be assertive, transgressive and a creature of passion, in other words bad, mad, or otherwise dangerous to know. It is worth noting, however, that both nineteenth-century reviewers and twentieth-century re-readers have tended to overestimate the *outspokenness* of sensation heroines, some of whom are remarkable for the power of a feeling which they are *unable to articulate*.

Contemporary reviewers tended to be most scandalized by the sensation novel's representation of the sensations of female passion. Margaret Oliphant, in one of several articles on the genre in *Blackwood's*, protested that:

> What is held up to us as the story of the feminine soul as it really exists underneath its conventional coverings, is a very fleshly and unlovely record.

Since the advent of sensationalism, she argued, the heroines of English fiction have been:

> Women driven wild with love for the man who leads them into desperation...Women who marry their grooms in fits of sensual passion...who pray their lovers to carry them off from husbands and homes they hate...who give and receive burning kisses and frantic embraces, and live in a voluptuous dream...the dreaming maiden waits. She waits now for flesh and muscles, for strong arms that seize her, and warm breath that thrills her through, and a host of other physical attractions....[W]ere the sketch made from the man's point of view, its openness would at least be less repulsive. The peculiarity of it in England is...that this intense appreciation of flesh and blood, this eagerness of physical sensation, is represented as the natural sentiment of English girls, and is offered to them not only as the portrait of their own state of mind, but as their amusement and mental food.[29]

Oliphant's outraged femininity, particularly in the latter part of the above extract, also gives a clue to another important element in the sensation novel's capacity to ruffle the feathers of respectable Victorian society: that is, the central part played by women in the production and mediation of the genre as both writers and readers. As one retrospective survey of the novels of the 1860s put it:

> A phalanx of lady-writers sprang up...armed with the 'Newgate Calendar', the Annals of the Divorce Court, the gossip of the smoking-room, the *argot* of the racecourse...Formerly we respected and admired our wives and sisters all the more for their innocent ignorance on certain topics, and now the most rustic maiden of sixteen, may by a diligent perusal of the works of her literary sisters, attain an almost perfect knowledge of every vice that festers beneath the sun.[30]

THE CULTURAL MEANING OF THE SENSATION GENRE

Genre is a socio-historical as well as a formal entity. Transformations in genre must be considered in relation to social changes.[31]

The title of this section, like the title of this book, names a category of fiction whose distinctive features I have attempted to sketch out in my opening section. This act of naming and defining a genre involves an attempt to fix something which might more usefully be seen as flexible and changing, as a process rather than an object. Fredric Jameson and Tzvetan Todorov (who is quoted at the head of this section) have both argued persuasively that genre is a social practice as well as a literary category, a 'socio-symbolic message'[32] which should be seen as a flexible and historically changing set of codes rather than as a fixed formula. My own approach follows Jameson by attempting to offer an historicized reading of the sensation novel as a process, a socio-symbolic message. However, ironically, as a first step towards understanding the cultural significance of this genre I must note that it was precisely the (perceived) fixed and formulaic quality of sensation novels upon which the contemporary critical debate about sensation fiction tended to focus.

Each game is played with the same pieces differing only in the moves. We watch them advancing through the intricacies of the plot, as we trace the course of an x or a y through the combinations of an algebraic equation.'[33]

Critics of the formulaic and mechanical nature of the style, structure and content of the sensation novel generally attributed it to contemporary developments in literary production, distribution and mediation. Many (perhaps most) early commentators on the sensation novel tended to focus on it as a commodity in an increasingly commercialized literary marketplace, which was debauched by the 'violent stimulant of serial publication' in periodicals.[34] An increase in literacy and, to some extent, a growth in the leisure-time in which to read led to a proliferation of tales of 'the marketable stamp',[35] which appeared first as serial instalments in periodicals and subsequently in three volume versions that were mainly issued through the circulating libraries. The spread of railway travel was another significant factor in developing the market conditions for sensation fiction. The sensation novel was, on the face of it, the ideal product for the railway bookstall, offering 'something hot and strong' to entice the 'hurried passenger' and relieve the dullness of the journey.[36] Mass-produced for mass consumption, the sensation novel was used by some critics to mark the boundary between high art and the popular artefact. Unlike the productions of high culture, it was argued, sensation novels were not written to 'satisfy the unconquerable yearnings of the [artist's] soul', rather they were (as H.L. Mansel put it) produced by the 'market law of supply and demand' and were 'redolent of the manufactory or the shop'.[37]

Although many contemporary reviewers insisted that the predictable and formulaic nature of the sensation novel made it a sterile form, it seems clear (at least with hindsight) that sensation fiction's power to disturb derived substantially from its adventurous and opportunistic mixing of formulas, and its blurring and crossing of generic, stylistic and other boundaries. The sensation novel's roots lie in a wide range of popular forms such as the Gothic novel, which flourished at the turn of the eighteenth and nineteenth centuries, Newgate tales of crimes and criminals, penny magazines, broadsheet street literature, stage melodrama and sensational journalism, as has been well documented.[38] Indeed, much of the energy and excitement of the sensation novel comes from the way it commandeered and reworked the subject matter and conventions of popular lower-class genres which had grown up alongside the dominant forms of middle-class fiction, but independent of the constraints of middle-class moral management. Written by middle-class authors, addressed (in the main) to middle-class and lower middle-class readers and often published in middle-brow journals, the sensation novel nevertheless cut across class boundaries and, much to the dismay of contemporary reviewers, it appeared to succeed in 'making the literature of the kitchen the favourite reading of the Drawing room'.[39] Other commentators were more worried about traffic in the other direction, and feared that the pernicious nonsense of sensationalism was passing from the parlour to the kitchen and turning the working classes into revolutionaries. In short, sensation fiction disturb-

12

ingly blurred the boundaries between the classes, between high art, low art and no art (newspapers), between the public and the private, and between the respectable and low life or *demi-monde*.

Sensation fiction was thus both the product and symptom of quite profound changes in fiction and the fiction market in the mid-Victorian period. The sensation debate and the sensation novel itself were also the focus for a range of interrelated social tensions and anxieties. The plots and central preoccupations of sensation novels embodied and, to some extent, explored the hopes and fears of Victorian middle classes. They were generated by a range of interconnected anxieties arising from contemporary social changes and the attendant challenging and questioning of the social and moral *status quo*. The chief of these anxieties concerned the nature and status of the family, generally considered to be the cornerstone of Victorian society, perhaps even of civilization itself. Sensation novels are almost always stories of a, or even *the*, family and their plots habitually reveal and exploit the fear that the respectable Victorian family had some dark secret at its core. In addition to this primal fear about the nature of the family, sensation fiction also articulates a range of anxieties arising from changes (or threatened changes) to the organization of the family. Gender roles are central here, and uncertainties about gender roles within the family, the differing expectations about marriage held by men and women, and misunderstandings between marital partners are a recurring theme. The issue of women's role within the family and beyond its boundaries was of particular importance. The Woman Question and the question of woman are central preoccupations of this genre, as I have argued elsewhere.[40] At a time when women and other reformers were clamouring for a widening of women's legal rights and educational and employment oppor-tunities, sensation novels reproduced and negotiated broader cultural anxieties about the nature and status of respectable femininity and the domestic ideal. Both implicitly and explicitly these novels raise questions about gender identity, and they both work with and rework prevailing gender stereotypes, such as the 'fast woman' the 'Girl of the Period', the 'Angel in the House', the 'manly man' and the feminized male who lacks a clear social role. Another area of anxiety about the family is manifested in the sensation novel's preoccupation with legal matters, particularly the role of the law in organizing and controlling the family. This is evident in the sensation novel's obsession with complex legal plots to do with wills and the inheritance of property, with the laws of bigamy and divorce, and with issues arising from women's lack of legal identity and rights (for example, the inability of married women to own property, and the inequitable nature of the divorce and child custody laws).

Another preoccupation of the sensation novel, complexly intertwined with the other issues and anxieties mentioned above, is social class. Questions of class and the relations between the classes, and a 'social paranoia about infiltration'[41] at a time of great social mobility figured prominently in the sensation novel as well as in the debate about it. As Dallas Liddle has noted, the thrills of the sensation novel derived in part from the way in which its characters and plots 'implied that both personal and class identity in contemporary Britain were fluid and unstable rather than secure, and thus potentially subject to manipulation, misrepresentation and outright theft'.[42] Many sensation novels dramatize and explore tensions between a declining landowning class (representative of an older, aristocratic order which is passing away) and a mercantile and professional bourgeoisie which is in the process of gaining political power and moral authority. Indeed, Jonathan Loesberg links the rise of the sensation novel in the 1860s to the debate about political reform leading up to the Reform Act of 1867. Related to concerns about social mobility and unstable class identities is an anxiety about moral authority and the sustainability of prevailing social and moral codes (the issue of propriety); many sensation novels turn on threats to the middle-class values of work and personal and family responsibility. Another important concern in sensation fiction is property, portable and otherwise. Financial insecurity, fears about the chimerical nature of Victorian speculative capitalism, and fears that the solid material comforts of well-to-do middle-class life might have all too insubstantial a base are played out in numerous plots concerning fraud and bankruptcy.

In its mixing of the mundane and the marvellous, the ordinary and the fantastic the sensation narrative became a distinctive form or mode for articulating the irrational and/or supra-rational in a materialistic, secular age. In this last respect, as in so many others, the sensation narrative demonstrates its affiliations with melodrama, one of the dominant cultural codes of the nineteenth century. Indeed, an important dimension of the cultural meaning and significance of the sensation narrative and the sensation genre is that it is a particular manifestation of 'the melodramatic imagination'[43] or the 'melodramatic mode', which, as Elaine Hadley has argued in *Melodramatic Tactics*, emerged in the early and mid-nineteenth century as 'a polemical response to the social, economic, and epistemological changes that characterized the consolidation of market society ...[and] the varied effects of the classificatory procedures instituted by English bureaucracy'.[44] Although originating in the theatre, as Hadley argues, the melodramatic mode was not confined to it:

> Melodrama's familial narratives of dispersal and reunion, its emphatically visual renderings of bodily torture and criminal conduct, its atmospheric menace and providential plotting, its expressions of highly charged emotion, and its tendency to personify absolutes like good and evil were represented in a wide variety of social settings, not just on the stage.[45]

Peter Brooks has also attributed the pervasiveness of the melodramatic imagination in nineteenth-century Europe to rapid social change and ideological crisis. In such conditions, he suggests, the melodramatic imagination performs a range of ideological work, functioning either as subversive critique or escapist entertainment. In nineteenth-century Britain, as Martha Vicinus[46] has noted, melodrama served as a 'cultural touchstone' for those classes or social groupings adrift on the sea of social change, and confused or ambivalent about their new role in the emerging social order, and as a 'psychological touchstone' for those who felt themselves to be 'helpless and unfriended', such as the poor and the powerless.

The sensation novel shares the stage melodrama's 'strong emotionalism; moral polarization and schematicization; extreme states of being, situations, action; overt villainy, persecution of the good, and final reward of virtue; inflated and extravagant expression; dark plottings, suspense, breathtaking peripety'.[47] Like the stage melodrama, the sensation novel also tends to displace social and political anxieties into emotional dramas

15

focused on the family. However, whereas in the domestic melodrama of the popular stage an idealized family was represented as the only sure refuge from threatening social upheavals, in the family romance of the sensation narrative the family is merely an illusory sanctuary, and is all too often the source of threatening upheaval.

The sensation novel has been regarded, almost from the moment of its inception, as a minor, marginal and short-lived form. Sensation novels, observed Henry Mansel, had a butterfly existence:

> Written to meet an ephemeral demand, aspiring only to an ephemeral existence...they...have recourse to rapid and ephemeral methods of awakening the interest of their readers, striving to act as the dram or the dose, rather than as the solid food.[48]

On the whole, literary history has tended to confirm Mansel's judgement. Until the last third of the twentieth century most sensation novels had disappeared from critical view. This was particularly true of the women's sensation novel, perhaps unsurprisingly given the greater propensity for popular texts by women writers to sink without trace within a generation of their first appearance. For much of the twentieth century Collins continued to be in demand with readers, and he was also afforded a place in an expanded canon of English literature as the father of the modern detective narrative. Ellen Wood's *East Lynne,* and Mary Elizabeth Braddon's *Lady Audley's Secret* persisted in the form of stage melodramas which remained a fairly constant part of the repertoire of the English theatre, and both were revived in the early 1990s. For most of the first two-thirds of the twentieth century, however, the sensation genre was regarded (if it was considered at all) as a historical curiosity, a mere episode in the fluctuating history of public taste, a genre so much the product of its particular historical moment that it was unable to survive that moment.

Sensation novels and sensation fiction were among the many texts and genres which were re-viewed in that process of reconfiguring the map of writing which resulted from both new empirical research and the theoretical developments of the 1970s. The work of reassessing sensation fiction was begun by Kathleen Tillotson and P. D. Edwards (in the essays to which I have already referred), who performed a very useful service both in restoring particular sensation novels to critical view, and providing well-informed accounts of the nature and significance of an important literary phenomenon of the mid-nineteenth century. This work was continued in Winifred Hughes's investigation of the sensation genre in relation to mid-Victorian critical debates and literary practices. Hughes's study, published in 1980, gave considerable prominence to the women writers of sensation fiction, following Elaine Showalter's reassessment of them in 1978 (see Bibliography). These feminist re-readings of the sensation genre also provided a context for Jenny Bourne Taylor's perceptive reading of Wilkie Collins's use of the sensation narrative to negotiate the contradictions of contemporary discourses about consciousness, identity, and the social formation of the self.

Sensation fiction was also one of a number of cultural fields that was recovered and reassessed in the last third of the twentieth century by a newly constituted interdisciplinary field of historical cultural studies which rethought the relations between text and context, reflection and mediation, and production and reproduction. Cultural studies together with feminist studies profoundly changed prevailing conceptions of what is marginal and what is central, what is 'major' and what is 'minor', and, indeed, of the usefulness of these terms. They also led to a radical rethinking of the relationship of (or boundaries between) high and low (popular) culture. When it first appeared this book was part of the process of recovery and reconfiguration which it described. This process has continued to develop apace in the last two decades and as yet there is no sign that scholarly, critical interest in sensation fiction is decreasing. Indeed in recent years sensationalism, the sensation novel and individual sensation novelists have regularly featured as conference topics, and as the subject of journal articles and edited collections, as well as in university courses on nineteenth-century fiction, women's writing, popular fiction and the literature of crime and detection.[49] Many more sensation novels are now available in modern editions than there were in 1994; the 'canonical' sensation novels of Collins, Braddon and Wood are now available in critical editions from several publishers including Oxford University Press (the World's

17

Classics series), Penguin and Broadview, and Jennifer Carnell's Sensation Press provides annotated editions of many of Braddon's lesser known novels. There has also been a renewal of popular interest in sensation fiction, as I shall show in Chapter 4. Several sensation novels have been newly adapted for the stage (including an Andrew Lloyd Webber musical based on *The Woman in White*), for screen (television and cinema) and for radio. Sensation fiction has also provided inspiration for a number of current novelists who have reworked its plots, techniques and themes in nineteenth-century settings, but from a twentieth- or twenty-first-century perspective.

Much of the critical work on sensation fiction that has appeared since 1994 has continued to focus on its trangressiveness, feminist rebelliousness and subversion of orthodoxy, or alternatively (mainly by those of a Foucauldian persuasion) on its disciplining of potentially unruly Victorian subjects and its management and containment of subversiveness and rebellion. Either way, critics and cultural historians have continued to mine the sensation novel for what it reveals of the political, sexual, racial and imperial unconscious of the culture of which it was a part, and to read and re-read sensation novels as 'tales obsessed with the others of Victorian society – deviant women, criminals, the lower classes, homosexuals, racial and cultural outsiders'.[50] However, there has also been a move beyond reductive readings of sensation novels as either simply radical or countercultural on the one hand, or cravenly or insidiously conservative on the other, towards an investigation of sensation fiction (often from an interdisciplinary perspective) as an inextricable component of Victorian culture, a site of 'contestation and negotiation of the debates surrounding gender, class and national and sexual identities during the Victorian period'.[51]

One of the more interesting developments has been the exploration of the sensation novel as an articulation of modernity. As Jenny Bourne Taylor reminded us in *The Secret Theatre of Home*, for Victorian critics the very word sensation 'encapsulated the experience of modernity itself – the sense of continuous and rapid change, of shocks, thrills, intensity, excitement'.[52] Like Taylor, D. A. Miller's *The Novel and the Police* (also published in 1988) sought to historicize the sensation novel in terms of its articulation of the impact of modernity on sensory experience. Both Taylor (using nineteenth-century psychological theories and practices of psychiatric medicine) and Miller (deploying queer theory and Foucauldian concepts of discipline), read the sensation novel as being implicated in ways of domesticating, stabilizing or disciplining the modern nervous subject. Some recent historians of the genre have preferred to approach its representation and articulation of modern nervousness through Walter Benjamin's theorization of modernity and modernization. Nicholas Daly, for example argues in *Literature, Technology and Modernity* that the 'specifically modern nervousness' which critics such as Miller identify in sensation fiction is inextricably connected to the modernization of the senses which Benjamin argued accompanied the technological revolutions of the nineteenth century. Sensation fiction, Daly argues, is both a product of and contribution to the 'mechanization of everyday life' in the nineteenth century: 'form, whether that of the sensation novel or of the sensation drama, is itself brought up to speed, which in turn means that the reading or viewing process comes to make some of the same demands as the industrial task'.[53] The technological revolution which Daly sees as being most closely connected to the formation of the modern nervous subject and to the rise of the sensation novel is railway travel. The speeded up world of railway travel not only features prominently in sensation narratives (as many earlier critics have noted), but it also alters perceptions of time and space and brings new fears and shocks in the shape of railway accidents. From the outset (as already noted above) the reading of sensation fiction was described as a form of railway reading and many nineteenth-century commentators attributed its popularity to the wish of railway passengers to have some distracting reading for the journey. Daly, on the other hand, argues that railway travel and the reading of sensation novels are analogous experiences; both the passenger and the reader become blankly passive subjects and, at the same time overexcited and discomposed. Sensation fiction, Daly argues, thus 'synchronizes its readers with industrial modernity':[54]

> what the sensation novel was preaching to the nerves was a new time-discipline: to be immersed in the plot of a sensation novel, to have one's nerves quiver with those of the hero or heroine, was to be

19

wired into a new mode of temporality. Time consciousness would be recast as pleasurable suspense. [55]

Another notable recent development in the study of sensation fiction is the attempt to rethink the scope of the category or genre by expanding the corpus of the sensation novel and extending the period of its occurrence. For example, Andrew Maunder's multi-volume *Varieties of Women's Sensation Fiction, 1855–1890* reintroduces long-forgotten sensation novels by Florence Marryat (*Love's Conflict*, 1865), Felicia Skene (*Hidden Depths*, 1866), Mary Cecil Hay (*Old Myddleton's Money,* 1874), and Dora Russell (*Beneath the Wave*, 1878), and makes a case for a further expansion of the range of writers and texts to be included in studies of the genre. As well as looking again at *what* the sensation novel was and *who* the sensation novelists were, Maunder and others have also re-examined the question of *when* the sensation novel occurred. Noting that Collins and Braddon wrote several (in Braddon's case numerous) novels and tales of crime and bigamy for magazines 'long before they struck gold'[56] with *The Woman in White* and *Lady Audley's Secret* in the 1860s, Maunder points to many other examples of sensation novels published before the critical and moral panic about sensation fiction in the 1860s. These include novels such as Bulwer Lytton's *Lucretia* (1846), which is based on the true story of Thomas Wainwright the poisoner and forger, Sophia Crawford's bigamy novel *A Double Marriage* (1851), Noel Radcliffe's *The Secret History of a Household* (1855), Caroline Clive's tale of a virtuous wife murderer, *Paul Ferroll* (1855), Emma Robinson's *Mauleverer's Divorce* (1857) and Dinah Mulock Craik's *A Life for a Life* (1859).[57] Moreover, it is clear that although the intense critical furore about the sensation novel had died down by the end of the 1860s (or, perhaps, began to turn into a wider debate about naturalism, the fiction of sex and the dangerous effects of reading novels), 'sensation' continued to be used as a generic marker or evaluative term by reviewers. Sensation elements also persisted in novels well beyond the end of the decade of the sensation boom, in the novels of both Collins and Braddon, and also, Andrew Maunder has argued, in the emergence of a second generation of women sensation writers in the 1870s and 1880s, some of whom took 'a more daring position on sexual licentiousness in the suburbs and the sexual double standard'.[58]

As well as Broughton and Marryat, this second generation of sensationalists includes Helen Mathers, Lady Emma Wood, Anna Steele and May Crommelin (the Irish-born writer Maria Henrietta de la Cherois Crommelin, author of 'thrilling domestic dramas').

The rediscovery of a new set of 'forgotten sensationalists' has by no means distracted attention from the novelists who were variously credited with originating and/or dominating the genre; Collins, Braddon and Wood have been the subject of great deal of new textual, biographical, critical, and theoretical work, some of which has challenged their status as originators of sensation fiction. Among other things this work has thrown fresh light on their writing practices, the form and meanings of their novels, their place in the nineteenth-century literary marketplace and the role they played in developments in publishing through their work as editors of periodicals (Wood as editor of *Argosy* and Braddon of *Temple Bar* and later *Belgravia*), as journalists or contributors to periodicals (all three), their involvement in the newspaper syndicalization of fiction (Braddon and Collins), and the different ways in which they negotiated the challenge to the dominance of the circulating libraries and the passing of the three-volume novel towards the end of the century (Braddon and Collins).[59] Indeed we now have a fuller understanding of the place of these three writers in Victorian print culture, and also of how the sensation novel and sensation novelists more generally were published, consumed and received. In particular Deborah Wynne's *The Sensation Novel and the Victorian Family Magazine* (2001) has focused attention on how sensation novels were first published and read in family magazines in a complex intertextual relationship with the articles, illustrations, and advertisements which surrounded them. Matthew Rubery, in *The Novelty of Newspapers: Victorian Fiction After the Invention of the News* (2009), has explored the interrelationship between the plots of sensation novels and the concealed narratives in the personal advertisements in the periodicals in which they appeared. In *The Literary Lives of Mary Elizabeth Braddon* (2000) Jennifer Carnell has fleshed out the details of Braddon's simultaneous anonymous authorship of tales with copious amounts of 'crime, treachery, murder, slow poisoning and general infamy'[60] for working-class readers of

21

halfpenny magazines, alongside her sensation serials for middle-brow magazines, and Andrew King has re-read *Lady Audley's Secret* in the context of one of the places of its publication – the *London Journal*.[61]

In addition the nature and significance of the sensation debate has been reviewed. Building on Kate Flint's work, in 'The Woman Reader and the Opiate of Fiction',[62] on Victorian representations of the woman reader of fiction in terms of consumption and addiction, these metaphors and the associated metaphor of disease deployed by the anti-sensationalists have been extensively explored and analysed and linked to contemporary anxieties about the effeminization and corruption of the national and imperial character.[63] Jennifer Phegley, on the other hand, has mounted a persuasive challenge to the all-pervasiveness of this negative view of the woman reader, arguing that although it was undoubtedly 'a major defining force behind the divisions between low and high culture [and] the definitions of literary forms such as realism and sensationalism', it was countered by certain family magazines which empowered women 'to participate in professional critical discourse as both consumers and producers of literary culture'.[64] In particular, Phegley shows how during the first five years of Braddon's editorship (1866–71), *Belgravia*, sought to transform attitudes to both women readers and popular literature by 'imagining the woman reader as active, independent, and informed' and by 'redefining the genre of the sensation novel as realistic, artistic, and instructive'.[65]

Sensation novels themselves still offer an 'exciting read', although some of their 'thrilling' devices, their stereotypical characters and situations, and their rhetorical mannerisms may cause the sophisticated twenty-first-century reader to smile. Sensation novels also provide interesting reading. Sensation novels are of great interest to the student of narrative form. They are also of great interest to those who wish to explore the processes involved in demarcating the boundaries between high art and popular forms and the processes by which the components of a living culture are sifted and stratified into a hierarchy of value and become (or fail to become) part of what Raymond Williams has described as the 'selective tradition'.[66] These novels also offer an interesting way of 'reading' mid-

Victorian culture, since they were often very direct (and sometimes quite self-conscious) interventions in contemporary social debates. Sensation novels were both produced by and reproduced mid-century anxieties on a wide range of issues. When we look in more detail at the work of the sensation authors we shall see that even when its final inclination was to uphold conventional morality, the sensation novel also probed and questioned Victorian moral and social orthodoxies.

2

Wilkie Collins

> We live ... in an age eminently favourable to the growth of all *roguery* which is careful enough to keep up appearances. (*A* 810)

The Woman in White is, for many critics, the 'archetype of the genre' of sensation fiction,[1] and its author is the master of its characteristic form, the novel with a secret. Indeed, secretiveness is not simply the structuring principle of the sensation plot, it is also its origin, and subject. Like most sensation narratives, Collins's plots also relied heavily upon the combination of roguery, hypocrisy and concealment that, as the quotation from *Armadale* at the head of this chapter suggests, was at the centre of modern life. In his own day Collins was the sensation novelist who was most highly regarded by reviewers and commentators on the contemporary cultural scene. Recent critical reassessments of his work have tended to confirm this placing, and to endorse Collins's own claims to originality as a writer who, as he puts it in his preface to *Armadale* 'oversteps, in more than one direction, the narrow limits within which [critics] are disposed to restrict the development of modern fiction' (*A* 4). Certainly, Collins's self-justificatory prefaces to his novels suggest that he regarded his own fictional practice more seriously than some of his fellow sensationalists – whether as source of shocks and thrills, as social or moral critique, as metaphysical investigation, or as narrative form. Collins was the master of all of the main elements of the sensation novel: the construction and unravelling of an intricate, crossword puzzle plot, the atmospheric scene, the mysterious, prophetic dream, obsessive and disordered mental states, overtly respectable villains, and bold, assertive and/or devious and scheming heroines and villainesses. Moreover, his fragmented, multi-vocal narratives were among the boldest experiments with narrative form to be

24

found in the sensation mode.

Many of Collins's novels have remained firm favourites with readers. However, despite T.S. Eliot's praise for his work in the *Times Literary Supplement* in 1927,[2] for much of the first half of the twentieth century Collins was regarded 'as Dickens's rather lightweight protégé and dubious companion – an interesting figure in the development of genre fiction, but not really worth sustained academic study'.[3] However, from the late 1960s academic critics began to explore the ways in which Collins's narratives self-consciously unmasked the venality, deception, self-deception and self-seeking that lurked below the surface of Victorian propriety, and offered a critique of Victorian social and moral orthodoxies. Towards the end of the twentieth century Collins, like other sensation novelists, benefited from the renewed interest in popular culture and its relationship to 'high' culture. In particular historicized readings informed by psychoanalytic, semiotic and feminist theories focused on the ways in which his sensation narratives articulated, explored and interrogated the social and psychological processes by which Victorian social and moral orthodoxies were constructed and maintained. These historically contextualized and theoretically inflected readings focused on the ways in which Collins's sensation novels examine how individual identities are formed within specific cultural codes, most notably those relating to class, gender and, perhaps to a lesser extent, race, and also within particular social institutions such as marriage and the family. They also demonstrate how Collins's fictions are centrally concerned with the intervention of the law in each of these areas. The following sections will focus on these issues, and on Collins's preoccupation with problems of subjectivity and perception and with the instability of (modern) identity.

BASIL, HIDE AND SEEK, THE DEAD SECRET

In the view of many contemporary reviewers and subsequent literary historians the sensational success of Wilkie Collins's *The Woman in White* inaugurated the sensation fiction phenomenon. However, although that 'bitter term of reproach "sensation," had not yet been invented for the terror of romancers in the fifty-second year of this present century', as Mary Elizabeth Braddon put it in her 1864 novel *The Doctor's Wife*, 'the thing existed nevertheless in divers forms, and people wrote sensation novels as unconsciously as Monsieur Jourdain talked prose' (*DW* 11). One example of the 'divers forms' that sensation novels took in 'the fifty-second year of the present century' is Collins's second novel, *Basil*, which appeared in that year. Together with *Hide and Seek* (1854) and *The Dead Secret* (1857), *Basil* was one of three novels involving family secrets, mystery and suspense, all set in the present or recent past, which Collins published before he enjoyed major success with *The Woman in White*. This 'Story of Modern Life' (as the novel was subtitled) is an extremely powerful novel, as *Bentley's Miscellany* acknowledged when it reviewed *Basil* alongside Thackeray's *Henry Esmond*:

> 'Basil' – although a story of to-day, although all its accidental environments are of the most ordinary character, although the scene is laid in a scarce-finished suburban square... although some of the personages are nothing more romantic than London linen-drapers ...is a story remarkable for...its intensity – for the powerful excitement it must provoke in every breast... It is a story of love and hatred...The *intense* everywhere predominates...The fatality of the Greek tragedians broods over the drama. There is a Nemesis not to be escaped. The hero of the tale sees a pretty girl in an omnibus; and he – goes to his doom.[4]

Geraldine Jewsbury was, perhaps, more representative of the negative tone of most reviews of *Basil* when she described its power as being that of 'fever' and suggested that it was 'a demonstration in morbid anatomy' over which 'hung a close, stifling, unwholesome odour'.[5]

Basil is a generic hybrid which combines the thrills of Gothic with both domestic realism and an urban realism which makes use of 'the most ordinary street-sounds that could be heard and the most ordinary street-events that could occur' (as Collins puts it in his Letter of Dedication, *B* xxxvi). Like those of Collins's novels which were labelled as sensation novels in the 1860s, *Basil* is a tangled tale of secrecy, plotting, deception, jealousy, revenge and violence, which features a clandestine marriage, adultery and marital suffering – all placed in the modern, up-to-date setting of London and its brand new suburbs. It takes the form of the confessional narrative of an aristocratic young man who, having fallen in love with a lower-middle-class girl whom he meets on an omnibus, falls prey to her schemes and those of her father, the linen-draper Sherwin. Lured into a marriage which Sherwin requires him to keep both secret and unconsummated for a year, Basil is estranged from his own family and tortured with frustration at the terms of his marriage and jealousy of his wife's relationship with her father's clerk, Mannion. The latter, in a further twist of the plot, is revealed to be the son of a disgraced former business associate of Basil's father. Basil's bizarre situation is shown as threatening his sense of personal and social identity and his sanity. His narrative is presented as his attempt both to understand himself and his history and to provide a warning to others.

Basil explores the 'formation and breakdown of the codes that shape masculine upper-middle-class identity',[6] by focusing on the way in which the conflicted and precarious masculine identity of the central protagonist is formed by his reaction to his father's and his brother's conceptions of aristocratic masculinity on the one hand, and, on the other, by his complex responses to different versions of femininity. Basil is both formed and alienated by his father's obsession with his family's ancient noble lineage and with social forms, and by the example (which Basil deplores) of his older brother's licentiousness and rejection of social forms. He is also presented as forming his own identity in relation to the highly idealized version of femininity personified by his sister Clara and his nervousness about a new troubling kind of modern femininity. For Basil, Clara is one of the guardians of 'that claim upon the sincere respect and admiration of men on which the power of the whole sex is based'. The power of this womanly ideal is seriously threatened in the present age,

> when too many women appear to be ambitious of morally unsexing themselves before society, by aping the language and manners of men – especially in reference to that miserable modern dandyism of demeanour, which aims at repressing all betrayal of warmth of feeling... Women of this exclusively modern order, like to use slang expressions... assume a bastard-masculine abruptness in their manners, a bastard-masculine licence in their opinions... Nothing impresses or delights them in a hearty, natural, womanly way. (*B* 19–20)

This tension between the traditional domestic feminine ideal and a more insurgent modern femininity was to become a prominent feature of many of Collins's later novels. In *Basil*, Margaret Sherwin is an example of the modern woman who (paradoxically) unsexes herself by flaunting her sexuality, by conspiring with her father to trap Basil into a marriage which unsexes or unmans him by its 'humiliating terms of dependence and prohibition' (*B* 143), and by adopting a 'bastard-masculine licence' in her dealings with Mannion. In *Basil*, as in his later novels, Collins makes use of dreams both to underline his themes and to represent and explore the psychological conflicts of his characters. For example, the polarized versions of femininity, embodied in the fair-haired Clara and the dark-haired Margaret, and also Basil's conflicted gender identity and sexuality are represented in his dream of the dark and the fair women when he first falls in love with Margaret. In Basil's dream the fair woman descends from 'bright summits' and leaves 'a long track of brightness, that sparkled far behind her, like the track of the stars when the winter night is clear and cold', while the dark woman approaches from 'the dark wood...her eyes lustrous and fascinating, as the eyes of a serpent' (*B* 45). Ignoring the beckoning of the fair woman, Basil touches the hand of her dark alternative in a scene which prefigures, albeit in more highly-wrought form, the nervous thrill of Walter Hartright's first meeting with the woman in white:

> in an instant the touch ran through me like fire ... I was drawn along in the arms of the dark woman, with my blood burning and my breath failing me, until we entered the secret recesses that lay amid the unfathomable depths of trees. There she encircled me in the folds of her dusky robe, and laid her cheek close to mine, and murmured a mysterious music in my ear...I had forgotten the woman of the fair hills, and had given myself up, heart and soul, and body, to the woman from the dark woods. (*B* 46–7)

As well as exploring contemporary aspects of, and anxieties about, the formation of gendered identities, *Basil* also focuses on class identities. Indeed, its plot is driven by a new fluidity in and breaching of class boundaries, and by cross-class tensions and class resentment. The secret cross-class marriage between the upper-class man and the linen-draper's daughter is the result of a chance meeting on an omnibus, a distinctly modern and democratic mode of transport, which, as Basil notes, is the only 'sphere in which persons of all classes and all temperaments are so oddly collected together' (*B* 27). Basil's cross-class marriage is also the focus of Mannion's class resentment at the upper-class man who has stolen the woman he has come to regard as his prize for his many years of hard and thankless work for her father – just as Basil's father had stolen his father from him by delivering him up to the legal authorities.

In his representation of Basil's gender, sexual and class identities Collins begins to develop a way of representing the modern nervous subject, which he was to take further in Walter Hartright and Ozias Midwinter. For example, the narrative foregrounds the way in which Basil's senses are strained by his encounter with modernity, whether this takes the form of an omnibus journey or his first visit to the Sherwin's home in the new north London suburbs, in which everything was so 'oppressively new', like the 'brilliantly-varnished door' which 'cracked with a report like a pistol when it was opened', that 'the eye ached at looking at', a domestic scene in which there 'was no repose anywhere' (*B* 61). Basil's nervousness is exacerbated by the terms of his secret marriage, by Mannion's taunting, by 'the awful thrill of suspicion' (*B* 159) about Margaret's relationship with Mannion, and by his horror at the scene he overhears between them when he trails them to a hotel on the day before he is due to claim Margaret as his wife:

> I could neither move nor breathe. The blood surged and heaved upward to my brain; my heart strained and writhed in anguish... Whole years of the direst mental and bodily agony were concentrated in that one moment of helpless, motionless torment. (*B* 160)

Basil's heightened nervousness results in a violent attack on Mannion, which severely disfigures the clerk and makes Basil fear himself to be mad. Following his attack on Mannion Basil suffers a complete nervous collapse, from which he is rescued by the care of his sister, a personalized form of the domestic moral management offered by the private asylums to which Anne Catherick and Braddon's Lady Audley were to be consigned.

Basil's story of a life disrupted by love for a lower-class woman and rivalry with a lower-class man ends in the calm of the feminized and rural world of his 'last retreat, this dearest home' that he shares with his sister on the small Breconshire estate she has inherited from her mother (*B* 342). He retreats from his sufferings into the obscurity, retirement and peace of a domestic existence which, for many female characters in sensation novels as well as women in real life was, at worst, a scene of suffering and, at best, a state of dependence and restriction. Collins's novel represents the negative face of feminine domesticity through Basil's perception of the experience of one of the novel's other nervous subjects, his mother-in-law Mrs Sherwin, a forerunner of Mrs Wragge in *No Name,* but entirely unrelieved by the comic presentation of the later novel:

> The restless timidity of her expression; the mixture of useless hesitation and involuntary rapidity in every one of her actions – all furnished the same significant betrayal of a life of incessant fear and restraint...in that mild wan face of hers...*there*, I could see one of those ghastly heart tragedies laid open before me, which are acted and re-acted, scene by scene, and year by year, in the secret theatre of home. (*B* 75–6)

Like other sensation novelists, Collins was to return again and again to the 'ghastly heart tragedies...which are acted and re-acted...in the secret theatre of home' throughout his career.

Much less sensational than *Basil,* Collins's next novel *Hide and Seek* (1854) is, nevertheless, like its predecessor, concerned with the mysteries of identity. 'We are mysteries even to ourselves' (*H&S* 77), the narrator observes of Zack Thorpe, who, like Basil, becomes estranged from his over-bearing and (in this case) religious father. *Hide and Seek* is also concerned with family mysteries and secrets, in particular the mystery of the origins of Mary, a deaf and dumb girl adopted by the artist Valentine Blyth and his wife Lavinia after they had rescued her from a life of ill-treatment in a travelling circus. As the narrative unravels the mystery of Mary's parentage and the secrets of Zack's father, it becomes (like so many sensation narratives) the vehicle of an attack on both the snobbery and the tedium of respectable English middle-class life. The reviewer in the *Leader,* possibly George Eliot[7] conceded that although 'it wants a climax', the story of *Hide and Seek* had 'a certain complicated cleverness with enough of mystery and expectation to keep attention alive'.[8]

Collins's next novel of family secrets was much more dramatic and sensational with its Gothic setting at Porthgenna

Tower, a hint of ghosts, and two women with a secret, one of whom is a mysterious, unstable woman who adopts a number of disguises and different identities. Like *Hide and Seek, The Dead Secret* (1857) also turns out to be the story of an illegitimate daughter, Rosamond Treverton, whose birth-mother, Sarah Leeson, a lady's maid, continues to seek to conceal the child's real identity in order that she may continue to enjoy the class status to which she was elevated when Sarah's employer, Mrs Treverton, secretly took the child as her own. In what was to become a prominent trope of the sensation novel, Sarah Leeson hides the document which (we learn later) would reveal the truth of Rosamond's birth, and she subsequently engages in a series of subterfuges to conceal the document's existence when she discovers, some fifteen years after Mrs Treverton's death that Rosamond has married Porthgenna Tower's new owner. This novel with a secret is full of suspense as the reader has to reconstruct Sarah's story from gradually revealed evidence and also – in an anticipation of *The Woman in White* – make sense of the eccentric behaviour of this increasingly mentally distracted lower-class woman. Like *The Woman in White* the plot turns, in part, on the swapping of the identities of two women of different classes and on the role of a strong willed woman, Rosamond, who plays detective.

THE WOMAN IN WHITE

The Woman in White, which began its serialization in the first issue of Dickens's *All the Year Round* in November 1859, not only helped to give Dickens's new periodical a flying start, but it also launched a new phase of Collins's writing career and a new vogue for sensation fiction. When he came to write *The Woman in White* Collins had already experimented with a range of narrative forms in his stories for Dickens's *Household Words* as well as his earlier novels. *Basil,* for example, is a first person narrative which refers to the narrator's own journal and newspaper articles and concludes with a number of letters written some years after the events which form the main narrative. However, *The Woman in White* was Collins's most thoroughgoing departure from a single narrative focus to date.

It consists of a series of narratives by various actors in, and observers of, events, as well as journal entries and other documents which are ostensibly collected and 'edited' by Walter Hartright, and made to tell, among other things, 'the story of what a Woman's patience can endure, and of what a Man's resolution can achieve' (*WW* 5). This collection of narratives, like those of *No Name* and *The Moonstone*, originates in a legal lack; in this case it stands in for testimony in a court of law. It tells the story of how the protagonists (especially the editor/hero Walter Hartright) have acted on their own behalf to right various wrongs without the formal assistance of the law, since 'the Law is still... the pre-engaged servant of the long purse' (*WW* 5).

Marriage and the hierarchical, patriarchal, nuclear family (often in a deviant or disrupted form), together with the social, psychological, moral and legal institutions that sustain these cornerstones of respectable Victorian society, are at the centre of all of Collins's novels. *The Woman in White,* like Collins's other sensation narratives of the 1860s, charts the transitions and transactions, within and across generations, between various fatherless and/or motherless families en route to (re-)establishing the normative companionate two-parent family of the bourgeois domestic ideal; a social and emotional unit in which both husband and wife find their vocation and their gender identity. However, before this destination is reached, both marriage and the family and the gender roles which they reproduce, and by which they are reproduced, are subjected to rigorous scrutiny.

Like virtually all sensation novels, *The Woman in White* offers a critique of the mercenary marriage. Much of the plot revolves around Sir Percival Glyde's attempts to ensure that Laura Fairlie complies with her dead father's wish that she should marry him, and his subsequent machinations to obtain total control of her money and property. Although this particular mercenary marriage is associated with the dark plottings of a melodramatic villain – and his Italian accomplice, Count Fosco, one of the most insidiously fascinating villains of nineteenth-century fiction – it is in other respects far from extraordinary. As Marian Halcombe, Laura's half-sister, explains to Hartright early in the narrative, Laura is 'in the position of hundreds of other women, who marry men without being greatly attracted to them or greatly repelled by them, and who learn to love them (when they don't learn to hate!) after marriage instead of before' (*WW* 72).

In opposition to its mercenary marriage plot *The Woman in White* offers a counter-narrative, which is replicated in Victorian novels of all kinds; the story of how virtuous love outwits the 'long purse', and of the process by which the poor man who loves the rich lady overcomes the problems of his lowly social status, the wishes of the lady's family and also – in this particular case – the machinations of her apparently aristocratic and wealthy (but dishonest and increasingly desperate) suitor/ husband. This counter-narrative combines the quest and self-sacrificing tasks required of the hero of romance with the Victorian ethos of self-help. Before he wins her as his bride and returns with her to her family home, Collins's hero must rescue the heroine from the prison of her mercenary marriage, and together with her half-sister care for her in a chaste *ménage à trois* modelled on the lower-middle-class household.

Before he assumes the role of Laura's husband, Hartright is first required to occupy the roles of both father and brother, those crucial male relatives whose lack has made Laura particularly vulnerable to Glyde's schemes. Moreover, before the poor man can marry the lady she must be stripped of her property and the trappings of her class:

> Forlorn and disowned, sorely tried and sadly changed; her beauty faded, her mind clouded; robbed of her station in the world... the devotion I had promised... might be laid blamelessly, now, at those dear feet. In the right of her calamity... she was mine at last! Mine to support, to protect, to cherish, to restore. Mine to love and honour as father and brother both. Mine to vindicate through all risks and all sacrifices – through the hopeless struggles against Rank and Power. (*WW* 422)

Here, as is so often the case in the sensation novel, properly socialized masculinity is defined in relation to, even constructed upon, vulnerable, dependent femininity. Hartright hides Laura away, labours to provide for her, and ultimately seeks out her persecutor and harries him to the point of destruction. Hartright's reward in this sensation plot (as, indeed, in most Victorian novels) is both the girl and the money. Having thoroughly discredited the mercenary marriage Collins smuggles a version of it back in at the end, with Hartright as the husband of a Laura restored to her former beauty and to rather more than her former wits, and as the father of Laura's child, the heir to Limmeridge.

At the centre of Walter's narrative, as at the centre of all sensation novels, is a woman with a secret, or several women with secrets. The chief of these is Anne Catherick, the mysterious woman in white, who, in the startling sensation scene near the beginning of the novel, seems to step out of Hartright's night thoughts as he walks home across Hampstead Heath. The woman in white and the complex network of her relations with the other characters is used to raise questions about the ways in which social and sexual identities are constructed and the categories within which they are formed. This strange, deranged woman, and the way in which she is represented, present an interpretative problem for both the characters in the text and the readers of it. The presentation of the initial night-time apparition indicates the scope of this problem. Is she a ghost? Is she a street-walker? Is she mad or bad or a victim? Is she a lady? All of these questions run through Hartright's mind as 'every drop of blood in [his] body was brought to a stop by the touch of a hand laid lightly and suddenly on [his] shoulder' (*WW* 20).

> There was nothing wild, nothing immodest in her manner: it was quiet and self-controlled . . . not exactly the manner of a lady, and, at the same time, not the manner of a woman in the humblest rank of life . . . What sort of woman she was, and how she came to be out alone in the high-road, an hour after midnight, I altogether failed to guess. (*WW* 20–1)

For Hartright the meeting with this questionable woman, 'whose character, whose story, whose objects in life, whose very presence by my side . . . were fathomless mysteries to me' (*WW* 23), precipitates an identity crisis: 'It was like a dream. Was I Walter Hartright? . . . Had I really left, little more than an hour since, the quiet, decent, conventionally-domestic atmosphere of my mother's cottage?' (*WW* 23).

One of the reasons that the woman in white presents a challenge to Walter's identity is that her appearance both challenges and blurs the gender categories upon which masculine identity was constructed. Walter's divided response to the woman is indicative of the contradictions of her appearance.

34

Walter initially responds as a chivalrous gentleman to those aspects of her appearance which signify respectable, middle-class femininity: self-control, vulnerability, guardedness, 'loneliness and helplessness'. Having helped her to avoid recapture, he is racked with guilt that he has let loose that uncaged femininity that it is the duty of every respectable man to control.

At Limmeridge House, as the drawing master to two young ladies, one of whom bears an uncanny resemblance to Anne Catherick, Walter's identity crisis becomes more acute. Here in a house whose nominal head is an emasculated invalid (Laura's uncle), and whose most resourceful member is a masculinized woman (Marian Halcombe), Hartright occupies the feminized role of the socially inferior artist:

> I had long since learnt to understand...as a matter of course, that my situation in life was considered a guarantee against any of my female pupils feeling more than the most ordinary interest in me, and that I was admitted among beautiful and captivating women much as a harmless domestic animal is admitted among them. (*WW* 64)

Fathoming the mysteries of the dubious and deranged woman in white and working out her connection with Laura Fairlie, the pupil with whom he falls in love, becomes one of the means by which Walter's identity crisis is resolved, and by which he is fully socialized into a conventional masculine role. This is a matter of action, work and the discovery of a vocation. The process of Walter's masculine socialization begins with a period of self-imposed exile in a 'new world of adventure and peril' (*WW* 414) in Central America, where 'my will had learnt to be strong, my heart to be resolute, my mind to rely on itself' (*WW* 415). Walter, the feminized, artistic dilettante, forges his identity as a man and an Englishman by surviving 'death by disease... Indians...[and] drowning' (*WW* 415). On his return to England he is forced by love and trouble to 'act for myself' (*WW* 636), and to labour for love and money. In so doing he finds both a vocation and a social role. Ultimately, as the agent of Laura's restoration to a Limmeridge, freed from the enervation of its legitimate heir, and the moral degeneration of the illegitimate aristocrat who seeks to usurp it, and as the father of the new heir, Walter acts as the renovator of both the family and the landed gentry.

The close physical resemblance of Laura and Anne is central to the plot of *The Woman in White,* as is the fact that they are actually related. Their relationship as textual doubles is also central to the novel's investigation of the formation of gendered social and psychological identities. In its treatment of Laura and Anne, the novel both explores and exposes the ways in which genteel femininity is constructed. Anne, the hypersensitive female, wandering the borderlands of sanity and insanity, is Laura without the social and economic advantages. Laura, as the legitimate daughter of a gentleman, is brought up in an excessively protective atmosphere to occupy a passive, childlike and dependent role, first in the paternal home and later as the wife of one who claims aristocratic birth. The distracted state of Anne Catherick, the illegitimate daughter of a gentleman, who has inherited the nervous debility of her father's family, is in one sense merely a heightened form of Laura's genteel femininity. In Anne's case conventional feminine dependence and passivity, in the absence of the social and familial frameworks which usually produce and sustain it, becomes a form of illness, an aberrant psychological state.

Collins's narrative is structured so as to close the social and psychological gap between Laura and Anne. Stripped of her social and legal identity by Glyde's plotting, Laura is also stripped of her psychological identity. After her rescue from the asylum it appears to Walter as if Laura has indeed become Anne:

> The fatal resemblance which I had once ... shuddered at seeing, in idea only, was now a real and living resemblance which asserted itself before my own eyes. (WW 443)

The novel substitutes Laura for Anne, just as Glyde substitutes Laura for Anne in the lunatic asylum. Both before and after her incarceration, Laura's domestic situation is repeatedly compared with Anne's (and later her own) containment within the asylum. Amidst the stifling, enervated gentility of Limmeridge House, and the Gothic terrors of Blackwater Park, Laura is just as much a prisoner as she (or Anne) is in the asylum. Ironically, even when she is liberated from the asylum and her husband's tyranny into the care of Hartright and Marian, Laura is still subject to strict controls and is kept more or less a prisoner for her own protection. Indeed, the novel depends for many of its effects on the similarities between the domestic regulation of women in the household and the regime of moral management practised in the new Victorian asylums which were modelled on the genteel home.[9]

If the action of *The Woman in White* is structured in terms of what were to come to be regarded as the conventional sensation plot devices of conspiracy, incarceration, duplicity, the detective hunt, the mysterious woman, and so on, this action is in turn organized around a series of pairings (which recur in virtually all of Collins's sensation narratives): sanity/insanity, legitimacy/ illegitimacy, masculinity/femininity, genteel femininity/the fallen woman, the womanly woman/the unwomanly woman. The dynamic interactions of these paired terms drive Collins's sensation narratives, which, in many cases turn on or explore the ways in which the polarities are defined, and the confusions and ambiguities that lurk within them.

The borderline (and the borderland) between sanity and insanity lies at the heart of this novel as it does, in some sense, of all of Collins's sensation novels. One of the most interesting aspects of Collins's representation of this borderland in *The Woman in White* is its inversion of the dominant code. The classic nineteenth-century madwoman is the deviant, energetic woman who defies familial and social control. In *The Woman in White*, however, it is the passive, controlled, domestic women, Anne and Laura, who are 'mad'. The sanity/insanity pairing is closely allied to the femininity/masculinity pairing, since, in the medical or psychiatric discourse within which Collins is working, madness is defined in relation to ideas of femininity. Feeling, excess, emotionalism, irrationality, histrionics, the main indicators of insanity, were also signifiers of femininity. Madness in the nineteenth century was in many respects defined as a 'female malady'.

The Woman in White, like all of Collins's novels (indeed, like all sensation novels) is shot through with anxieties and ambiguities about the masculinity/femininity pairing. It focuses on the blurring of the boundary between these two terms and exposes the ways in which this boundary is constructed within specific codes of representation and perception. Thus the reader's perception of Marian Halcombe's 'masculinity' is, in large measure, a product of Hartright's conventional perceptual framework through which Marian is mediated. Hartright sees Marian's body as a model of female beauty, but her 'large, firm, masculine mouth and jaw', swarthy complexion, dark down on the upper lip, 'prominent, piercing, resolute brown eyes' all signify masculinity. Even more alarming, 'her expression – bright, frank, and intelligent – appeared, while she was silent, to be altogether wanting in those feminine attractions of gentleness and pliability' (*WW* 32). What is attractive in a woman is, in terms of the dominant codes of representation, repulsive in a man. Hartright's perception of Frederick Fairlie, Laura's uncle, is the logical extension of his view of Marian. His 'beardless face', 'effeminately small feet', 'little womanish' slippers, and 'frail, languidly-fretful, over-refined look' had 'something singularly and unpleasantly delicate in its association with a man' (*WW* 39).

The perceptual codes by means of which gender difference is constructed are also explored via Marian Halcombe's diaries. Here the world is viewed through the eyes of a woman who questions and refuses the dominant codes. Marian chafes under the restraints of her 'petticoat existence', fulminates against men as 'the enemies of our [women's] innocence and our peace', and observes with a critical and knowing eye the transformation (by a man and marriage) of the vain, opinionated Eleanor Fairlie to a 'civil, silent, unobtrusive woman, who is never in the way' (*WW* 219). Through Collins's use of different narratorial perspectives we are confronted with different ways of seeing gender difference. This creates a space in which the reader can see that these are, for the most part, *just* ways of seeing: gender is not something natural and fixed, rather it is produced and subject to change. This recognition is either immensely liberating, or it induces deep anxiety, depending on the reader's point of view. However, in the end, the subversive potential of the juxtaposed narratives is (on the whole) contained and the culmination of the narrative and Walter's narrative control restores a normative view of masculinity/femininity. The world of *The Woman in White* seems to be one in which the relation between masculinity and femininity has somehow gone wrong. It has both masculinized women and feminized men, but mostly there is just too much femininity around, and where there is masculinity it occurs in inappropriate places. One of the things that Collins's narrative does is to redress this gender imbalance.

Another imbalance that is redressed in *The Woman in White* is that between legitimacy and illegitimacy. This particular pairing, like the others in this novel, is inextricably tied up with the question of gender and gender stereotypes. The key figure here is the fallen woman, since illegitimacy, by definition, involves an unmarried mother or a married woman who has a child that is not her husband's. The plot of *The Woman in White* originates in illegitimacy: the illegitimacy of Glyde and of Anne Catherick. Mrs Catherick, a fallen woman, is the link between the different plot strands. Again there is the suggestion of a disruptive femininity let loose on the world. As in so many sensation novels, one of the narrative goals of this novel is to (re-)establish the (legally) legitimate succession, and to establish its moral legitimacy. Thus, at the end of the novel, the legal heirs of Limmeridge succeed to what is rightfully theirs. 'Succeed' and 'rightful' here have a moral as well as a legal meaning: they have succeeded by their own efforts, and their right is that of moral authority. Squaring the circle of moral and legal legitimacy and containing disruptive femininity is also a major concern of Collins's next novel, *No Name*.

NO NAME

In *The Woman in White* the marriage and property laws are used and manipulated to strip the heroine of her property, status, and even her identity. In *No Name* it is the 'heroine', if one may use this term for its transgressive central female character Magdalen Vanstone, who resorts to marriage scheming in order to regain the name and property which the law has taken away. Like its predecessor *No Name* originates in a crisis of legitimacy, and foregrounds the problematic legal status and economic dependency of women.

In *No Name* the Vanstone family is quite literally destroyed when the sudden deaths of their parents reveal Norah and Magdalen Vanstone to be illegitimate. The death of Mr Vanstone's legal wife, a disreputable woman who had tricked him into marriage when he was a young soldier in Canada, had finally permitted the Vanstone parents to legalize their union only weeks before they themselves met with unexpected deaths following a railway accident. Like Sir Percival Glyde, whose secret illegitimacy is a powerful narrative force in *The Woman in White*, the Vanstone sisters have no legal right to their name, their place in society, or their father's property, which, because of a legal nicety about the dating of a will, passes to an unsympathetic male relative. The Vanstone sisters are the victims of what Miss Garth (their former governess) describes as 'a cruel law', which 'visits the sins of the parents on the children', and is 'a disgrace to the nation' (*NN* 138).

Collins's preoccupation with illegitimacy and inheritance may be explained, in part, by the irregularity of his own domestic arrangements; he never married, but maintained separate households with Caroline Graves and Martha Rudd (also known as 'Mrs Dawson'), the mother of his three children.[10] However, this preoccupation with illegitimacy and inheritance is also part of a more general investigation in Collins's fiction of the ways in which the law's intervention in family life defines and restricts those whom it claims to protect – especially women.

The opening chapters of *No Name* offer a picture of domestic bliss and well-ordered family life which is destroyed by the discovery that the Vanstones were not in fact married for almost all of the twenty-seven years of their partnership. The almost perfect happy family to which the reader is introduced in the early chapters is revealed retrospectively to be no family at all in the legal sense. Thus, from the outset, a tension is set up between the idea of the family as an affective emotional space, and as a socio-legal institution. The discovery of the legal irregularity also casts the shadow of impropriety over a family which has hitherto been a model of respectability. This plot device triggers an exploration and interrogation of the codes of propriety and respectability, which is an important part of this novel's project.

The sudden shift in family fortunes at the beginning of this narrative is a common device in sensation fiction and derives from a broader cultural anxiety about the stability of the family. This anxiety is partly economic: the women sensation novelists in particular were very preoccupied with the financial insecurities of the higher classes of society. It is also based on mid-century uncertainties about the nature, structure and function of the family as a social institution. Even before the revelations which destroy the Vanstone family there are indications of familial instability and disturbance in Magdalen's excess of feeling, her impulsiveness, her disregard for social proprieties, her delight in exercising her talent for acting, and her playful subversion of her father's authority. In short, from the outset disruptive femininity threatens the family. There is an interesting displacement at work here. On one level Collins's narrative makes it clear that the disaster which befalls the Vanstone sisters is the result of an unjust law and the selfishness of a male relative. However, the novel's focusing on Magdalen's excessive emotions and her scheming also has the effect of transferring the reader's attention, and perhaps also the blame for the family's predicament, to her perverse femininity and her obsessive desire for revenge and restitution.

Magdalen is a particularly striking example of the sensation novel's concern with – or perhaps it would be more accurate to describe it as an anxiety about – feminine duplicity. At times it seems as if the sensation novel in general *defines* femininity as duplicity and represents respectable, genteel femininity as impersonation, performance or masquerade. This novel uses acting as a general metaphor for social existence. It also explores the complexities and problems of a concept of identity based on performance. The novel's preoccupation with performativity and theatricality is also evident in its organization as a series of directly narrated 'Scenes' which are punctuated by sections entitled 'Between The Scenes', which are made up of letters and extracts from journals.

Magdalen is represented as a 'natural' or 'born' actress whose 'habits of mimicry' (*NN* 17) and talent for acting (demonstrated in the private theatricals in chapters 5 and 6) are linked to her vivacity and love of sensation:

> I want to go to another concert...anything that puts me into a new dress, and plunges me into a crowd of people, and illuminates me with plenty of light, and sets me in a tingle of excitement all over, from head to foot. (*NN* 16)

A sensation seeker whose behaviour often causes a sensation,

Magdalen is a prototype of the 'girl of the period', a term coined by the journalist and novelist Eliza Lynn Linton to describe the restless modern woman who seeks a wider scope for her life, and more independence, activity and pleasure than was usually permitted to the respectable middle-class woman. When she is deprived of her legal identity and her place in respectable middle-class society, Magdalen both reacts and acts: she reacts with violent emotion to injustice, and she acts in the sense of taking positive steps to deal with her changed circumstances. She does not merely regret the restraints of petticoat existence, as Marian Halcombe does, she refuses to accept them. She is the antithesis of the respectable feminine ideal, personified by the passive, accepting Laura Fairlie and by her own sister Norah. She is 'resolute and impetuous, clever and domineering... not one of those model women who want a man to look up to and protect them' (*NN* 77) – although, of course, before her drama is played out Collins's narrative will require her to be saved from her own excesses and to rely on the protection of a strong man.

Magdalen adapts to the loss of her original social status by learning to control her nervousness, transgressing the code of propriety and working as a professional actress in the public theatre. Subsequently, at first under the direction of Captain Wragge and then on her own behalf, Magdalen exchanges the social and moral ambiguity of the role of the professional actress for the fluid identity and role playing of the swindler who attempts to regain her father's fortune for herself and her sister by duping his legal heirs. In Magdalen, Collins creates a character who demonstrates the instability of the particular conception of (respectable, middle-class) feminine identity which underpins the dominant code of social propriety, and also the contradictions inherent in that code. Magdalen performs this function by self-consciously exploiting her perception that 'a lady' is simply 'a woman who wears a silk gown, and has a sense of her own importance' (*NN* 613). In one sense Magdalen's scheming is but a heightened version of the machinations in which thousands of middle-class women (and men) engaged in order to make a good marriage: 'Thousands of women marry for money' she asserts, 'Why shouldn't I?' (*NN* 489). Indeed, through scheming and impersonation, and by making 'the general sense of propriety my accomplice' (*NN* 590),

Magdalen does succeed in acquiring, if only briefly, a legitimate social identity:

> I am a respectable married woman...I have got a place in the world, and a name in the world, at last. Even the law which is the friend of all you respectable people, has recognised my existence, and has become my friend too...my wickedness has made Nobody's Child, Somebody's Wife. (*NN* 590)

Two things distinguish Magdalen from her sister Norah and the thousands of other 'respectable' women (less noble than the saintly Norah) who play the required social role and succeed in marrying for money. One is the extraordinarily self-conscious exploitativeness of her performance, the other is the multiplicity of parts she plays. These two distinguishing characteristics are the marks of Magdalen's excess and perversity noted earlier. In Collins's representation of Magdalen, the histrionic and the hysterical are closely connected: her acting is both produced by and induces hysteria, that excessive emotional state into which, according to nineteenth-century medical discourse, all women were perpetually in danger of falling.

Collins's narrative is driven by the nervous energy of Magdalen's transgressive excess. Norah's 'story', on the other hand, demonstrates that, in sensation novels at least, good women do not have a story, they inhabit a sub-plot. However, if Magdalen's excess is the source of narrative, the curtailment of that excess is its end; that is to say it is both the goal of the narrative and its closure. Magdalen's adoption of multiple identities as the means of regaining (or possibly regressing to) her original identity results in self-fragmentation and a loss of social, legal and psychological identity. All of Magdalen's schemes are frustrated, and she retires from the fray penniless and exhausted. The final part of the novel depicts Magdalen's decline into a life-threatening collapse, the result, according to the doctor who is summoned to her side, of 'some long-continued mental trial, some wearing or terrible suspense... [under which her] whole nervous system has given way' (*NN* 704). Like Basil and Laura Fairlie, Magdalen is restored to health by a period of domestic confinement with Captain Kirke, the sailor whom she had unwittingly encountered at a crucial earlier stage in her moral development (or degeneration), and, coincidentally the son of her father's closest friend from his days in Canada. Like Basil's period of recovery with his sister, Magdalen's rest cure resembles the system of moral management in a domestic setting practised by the new asylums. Magdalen emerges from her illness not with a restored identity, but with an identity which has been reshaped by her recognition of herself as the woman who is loved by Captain Kirke, the man who nurses her with a woman's tenderness, and by her recognition of Kirke as the man she would have liked to have been: 'Oh, if I could be a man, how I should like to be such a man as this!' (NN 720). In her new identity Magdalen is restored to respectable society and reclaimed for the patriarchal family.

Magdalen is a particularly powerful version of the new self-assertive, independent heroine for which the sensation novel was renowned (or infamous). She is one of those 'bouncing, ill-conditioned, impudent young [women]', whose fictional rise Collins noted in 'A Petition to the Novel-Writers'.[11] Collins represents this new stereotype with an ambivalence which is characteristic of the sensation genre. Collins's text positions its readers so that we cannot entirely condone Magdalen, but nor can we unequivocally condemn her. Instead we are made into the spectators of her beauty and brilliance, and the witnesses of her emotional turmoil. Throughout the narrative Magdalen is defined as a woman of feeling. An excess of self-assertive, self-directed feeling is the origin of her moral decline. On the other hand, the vulnerable feminine sensitivity which follows her hysterical breakdown, and (finally) properly directed (hetero-sexual) feeling are the means by which she is reclaimed. I shall return to the matter of the representation and circulation of feminine feeling in the sensation novel, and some of the questions it raises, when I look at the female sensationalists.

Magdalen is only one of a number of distinctive modern types in No Name. The fluidity of her identity (or identities), her nervous energy and her susceptibility to hysteria make her, among other things, a version of the modern nervous subject. Another version of this phenomenon is provided in Noel Vanstone, Magdalen's cousin and briefly her husband. Queru-lous, effete, with a tendency to invalidism, this 'frail, flaxen-haired, self-satisfied little man, clothed in a fair white dressing gown', who has a complexion 'as delicate as a girls' (*NN* 281), displays, like Henry Fairlie in *The Woman in White*, a nervousness that is symptomatic of both degeneration and over-civilization. A distinctive modern type in quite a different mould is Captain Wragge, the self-professed swindler or 'moral agriculturalist' who cultivates and exploits 'the field of human sympathy' (*NN* 211) and practises his own particular form of redistributing wealth from those who have to those, like himself, who are able to get their hands on it by devious means. A striking illustration of the view that the mid-nineteenth century is 'an age eminently favourable to the growth of all *roguery* which is careful enough to keep up appearances' (*A* 657). Wragge, with his meticulously organized filing system and ordered set of accounts, together with his investments in Magdalen, railways, and finally a multipurpose pill, is both an example of the professionalization of roguery and a satire on Victorian social mobility by means of the culture of speculation.

ARMADALE

The transgressive heroine and the modern rogue are taken several stages further in Lydia Gwilt, the *femme fatale* villainess of *Armadale*, a novel about greed, cupidity, jealousy and fatalism, which was described by the *Athenaeum's* reviewer H.F. Chorley as 'a sensation novel with a vengeance' and the 'product of a diseased invention'.[12] The actions of Braddon's Lady Audley, hitherto the type of the beautiful and deceptively demure sensation villainess, pale into insignificance beside the passionate intensity and sophisticated, scheming criminality of Lydia Gwilt. This attractive governess, murderess, adulteress and forger is the extreme form of the demonic sensation heroine, 'at once passionate and cold-blooded, resolute and capable of murder'.[13] Her emotional intensity and her criminality are both concealed beneath the façade of the respectable Victorian lady.

> Perfectly modest in her manner, possessed to perfection of the graceful refinements of a lady, she had all the allurements that feast the eye, all the siren-invitations that seduce the sense – a subtle suggestiveness in her silence and a sexual sorcery in her smile. (*A* 462)

Once more the central female character of a sensation novel is double, and the novel exploits the fear that the self-sacrificing, passionless gentility which constitutes the feminine ideal is merely a form of acting or impersonation which masks female passion and self-interest. The story that this character attempts to write for herself is a ruthless self-help narrative aimed at securing a stable social and financial position by exploiting her sexual attractiveness, successfully impersonating respectable femininity and entrapping an unsuspecting man into marriage. The story that Collins writes for her involves the exposure of her impersonation and the revelation of the duplicity, intense passions and mysterious past which it masks. Collins does this by giving the reader a privileged access to his character's inner dramas by using Lydia's diary, and letters between Lydia and her partner in crime, the procuress Mother Oldershaw. These documents allow the reader to watch Lydia watching herself – the same effect is achieved by the use of Marian Halcombe's diaries in *The Woman in White*. They present the reader with a particular form of the self-surveillance upon which Victorian identity and morality were founded. In the letters, and more especially the diary, Lydia is revealed as a complex and contradictory mixture of calculating rationality and impulsive emotionalism, coolheadedness and obsessiveness, sexual desire and sexual disgust; for example, when she remembers her past history of sexual degradation. The letters and diary also chart the process by which Lydia develops the capacity for redemption. Once more feeling is the key. If misplaced (perverse) desire is the source of Lydia's transgressiveness, then, as her diary shows, properly directed feeling – spontaneous, romantic, heterosexual love – is the possible route to repentance. Lydia's love for Midwinter becomes a form of conscience. It not only deflects Lydia from her schemes, but it also deflects her from her self-obsession; the strong, resourceful, independent woman is made vulnerable and dependent by sexual desire and romantic love.

It is not possible, however, for the sensation novel to envisage the reincorporation into respectable society of a character whose criminality is as varied and as profound as Lydia Gwilt's. Many critics, including Margaret Oliphant, had been outraged by the rescue of Magdalen Vanstone from 'a career of vulgar and aimless trickery and wickedness', at the apparently 'cheap cost of a fever', from which she emerges 'as pure, as high-minded and as spotless as the most dazzling white of heroines'.[14] In *Armadale* the possibility of a moral redemption is signalled by the *femme fatale's* final act of self-sacrifice, when she saves Midwinter's life by sacrificing her own. In its fantasy resolution of the problem of the deadly woman, Collins's novel turns the destructive potential of transgressive femininity against itself.

Lydia Gwilt is at the centre of the narrative from which she is, in the end, violently expelled. Her own schemes and her association with such 'moral agriculturalists' as Mother Old-ershaw and Doctor Downward (also known as Le Doux), an abortionist turned proprietor of a sanatorium for nervous invalids, place her at the heart of Collins's critique of the cupidity, corruption and criminality which lurks within re-spectable Victorian society. As both victim and instigator, she is also at the centre of that network of surveillance and spying which the novel represents as a characteristic form of modern life. Spying and being spied on are among the dominant activities in sensation fiction. Spying is clearly the other side of the sensation novel's concern with secrecy, and its suggestion that everyone has something to hide. At the centre of the insidious and pervasive network of surveillance is

> the Confidential Spy of modern times...the necessary detective attendant on the progress of our national civilization...a man professionally ready on the merest suspicion (if the merest suspicion paid him) to get under our beds, and to look through gimlet-holes in our doors. (*A* 627)

Walter Benjamin described this fictional preoccupation with surveillance and detection, and the rise of the detective and detective fiction as symptoms of urban modernity. As he observes of nineteenth-century Paris: 'in times of terror, when everyone is something of a conspirator, everybody will be in a situation where he has to play detective'.[15]

Lydia Gwilt also has a crucial role in the fatal inheritance plot which gives rise to many of the novel's most thrilling sensation scenes. Many of the proliferating plots of this extremely complexly plotted novel radiate out from the story of family secrets which is told in the confessional narrative in the prologue. This prologue establishes the novel's concern with questions of identity, and with inheritance – of a name and property. It also raises questions about the determining influence of the familial past, whether through the transmission of degenerative physical and mental characteristics, or as a shaping destiny or fate. Indeed, Collins's explicit questioning of the extent to which lives are shaped by a predestined fate or by the specific actions and choices of individuals makes *Armadale* one of his most thoroughgoing explorations of issues of destiny and free will. The prologue tells a story of intra-familial conflict and murder in the form of the (dictated) confession of Allan Armadale to his son, also Allan Armadale. The dying Armadale (originally named Wrentmore) confesses to the murder of the man whose name he had been required to take as a condition of inheriting the Armadale property in England and Barbados. This confession is both a testament of guilt and a prophecy of the ineradicability of that guilt:

> I see danger in the future, begotten of the danger in the past – treachery that is the offspring of his treachery, and crime that is the child of my crime...I see the vices which have contaminated the father, descending and contaminating the child...(*A* 54–5)

The confession ends with a prophetic warning to his son:

> Avoid the widow of the man I killed...Avoid the maid whose wicked hand smoothed the way to the marriage...avoid the man who bears the same name as your own...hide yourself from him under an assumed name...be all that is most repellent to your own gentler nature, rather than live under the same roof...with that man. (*A* 55–6)

The reader of a psychoanalytic bent will no doubt find much to ponder in this Law of the Father which (as it turns out) forbids relationships with the very man and woman whom the son most desires. Indeed the relationship between Midwinter, Allan Armadale and Lydia Gwilt is an example of that homoerotic triangle – which Eve Kosofsky Sedgwick argued was a prominent feature of Victorian fiction – in which the sexual attraction of two men for each other is expressed or mediated through their relationship with a woman.[16]

The confession is given a central role in the novel's investigation of the processes by which identity and subjectivity are formed. When Wrentmore/Armadale's son reads these

48

words in the letter of confession that is part of his inheritance when he comes of age, they give a retrospective shape and meaning to the painful puzzle of his existence:

> there was I, an ill-conditioned brat, with my mother's negro blood in my face, and my murdering father's passions in my heart. (*A* 105)

By the time he reads his father's letter, the murderer's son has already changed his name to Ozias Midwinter in the course of a wandering self-exile from his family. The confession produces further complications in Midwinter's sense of identity. It leads to both a repudiation of self and an acceptance of the guilt and unworthiness which has been imposed upon him by his father. This re-formation of Midwinter's identity is also accompanied by a process of splitting. His knowledge of the guilty past, and his fears about its ability to shape the future lead Midwinter to spy upon himself, in other words to practice a form of that self-surveillance already noted in Lydia Gwilt.

Midwinter's hypersensitivity, his susceptibility to non-rational modes of interpretation, and his emotional self-policing combine to place him in a role in the sensation narrative which is more usually occupied by a female character – the hysteric. His hysterical symptoms are the result of a desire to repress and to control his fears and feelings (in other words, to be 'manly'). They are the result, too, of the withdrawal from emotional bonds which he imposes upon himself in an attempt both to outwit and to deny the versions of his history and destiny contained in his father's prophecy. Ironically, however, each time that Midwinter scores a 'victory over his own fatalism' he seems to open a door to further crime, and the Armadale curse seems to move one more stage towards fulfilment. The chief instigator of this crime is Lydia Gwilt, who as a 12-year-old servant had played a part in the dramas of the earlier generation of Allan Armadales. The repressed legacy of the past thus re-enters the narrative, as it so often does in sensation fiction, in the shape of a guilty, powerful and sexually desirable woman.

The cycle of guilt and treachery is only broken by means of Midwinter's confronting and expelling Lydia Gwilt and by his confronting and redirecting the feminine in himself – he 'take[s] to Literature' (*A* 814). In the process the links with the West Indies – represented in the prologue as a wild zone of dissolute youth, and financial and sexual speculation and intrigue – are finally severed. The novel seems to accept colonial guilt in its depiction of the cupidity and violence of white colonists, but it does so in a displaced form by associating that guilt with the 'idleness and self-indulgence' of Allan (Wrentmore) Armadale's 'wild' and 'vicious' period as a slave owner in the Barbados of the 1820s, where he is corrupted by his power over 'slaves and half-castes...to whom my will was law' (*A* 31). Collins's representation of the colonial past thus seems to suggest, that the supposedly civilized subjects of the colonizing power are themselves liable to be colonized by the primitive power of the people and lands they have colonized. It also suggests, as Lillian Nayder argues, that Collins seems to be 'more concerned with the corrupting effects of slavery on the plantation owners than with the suffering of the slaves'.[17] By the end of the narrative the name of Allan Armadale which has previously been in circulation in a different location and between different men becomes fixed to a member of the English aristocracy and owner of the thoroughly modern Thorpe Ambrose, 'a purely conventional country-house – the product of the classical idea filtered judiciously through the commercial English mind' (*A* 202). The novel's ending, like that of many other sensation novels, is *diminuendo*. It concludes with a peculiarly (and rather enfeebled) English tranquillity, with the wedding of Allan Armadale, a model of frank, open, English masculinity, to the ultra-feminine, respectably insipid, 'Neelie' Milroy.

THE MOONSTONE

The plot of *The Moonstone* like that of *Armadale* also originates in a tale of violence and greed in the colonies, and in the familial discord of an earlier generation. This tale is also told in a prologue, in this case in the form of a document from the Herncastle family papers which relates the history of the Yellow Diamond, 'a famous gem in the native annals of India' (*M* 1), and of its removal to England from its latest resting place in Seringapatam. As in *Armadale*, the main narrative of *The Moonstone* concerns the disruption of the tranquillity and order of genteel English life by a colonial legacy. The Diamond and its attendant burdens are left to Rachel Verinder in the will of her uncle, who had plundered the Diamond in battle. This legacy is intended as an act of vengeance against the family which had ostracized him. In the 'political unconscious' of this text[18] Rachel's inheritance of the Diamond also signifies the inescapability and pervasiveness of the burden of colonial guilt; even genteel young women are implicated in the white man's burden, and the consequences of colonial plunder surface in the English country house. As the loquacious Gabriel Betteredge, the Verinder's loyal family servant puts it:

> here was our quiet English house suddenly invaded by a devilish Indian Diamond... Who ever heard the like of it – in the nineteenth century mind; in an age of progress, and in a country that rejoices in the blessings of the British constitution. (M 67)

This, the most domestic of Collins's novels, involves a crime at the very heart and hearth of the family. Indeed there has been some debate as to whether *The Moonstone* should be considered as a sensation novel at all, or whether it should more properly be seen as a prototype of the detective novel, and one of the earliest occurrences of the English Country House Mystery. Certainly it has many of the features that became staple ingredients of the Country House Mystery: the crime is committed at a family gathering – the celebration of Rachel's birthday – which brings together a mixed group of people, many of whom might have a motive for committing the crime; it has suspicious servants; there is a bumbling local policeman (Seegrave) whose dullness of wit and lack of gentility render him quite unequipped to decipher the codes of the genteel household; and a detective of repute (Cuff), more used to the ways of the gentry, is brought in to apply his specialist intuitive as well as deductive skills to the mystery (only in this case he comes to the wrong conclusion in the first instance).

Whatever its claims to be the prototypical English detective novel, *The Moonstone* certainly has many of the key components of the sensation novel: (1) it makes use of dreams and altered states of consciousness; (2) it produces thrills by means of atmospheric writing – most notably in the descriptions of the Shivering Sand; (3) it turns on a mystery from the past; (4) family secrets lie at its centre; (5) there is a marriage plot and fraud, both perpetrated by the same individual; (6) there is a minute focus on the domestic space and domestic relations; (7) the amateur detective is a young man (Franklin Blake) with foreign tastes and no clearly defined social role, and hence no clearly defined gender role; (8) a crucial part is played by a woman with a guilty past and a present secret – Rosanna Spearman, who has been imprisoned for theft, and who cherishes a hopeless love for a man who is her social superior; (9) the narrative is kept in motion by a woman with a secret (Rachel Verinder); (10) female passions propel the narrative, and female passions and physical sensations are minutely described.

Rachel Verinder, as Collins's preface emphasizes, is at the centre of *The Moonstone:* 'the conduct pursued, under a sudden emergency, by a young girl, supplies the foundation on which I have built this book' (*M* liv). The theft of the Diamond disrupts the Verinder household and gives rise to the 'detective fever' around which the plot is constructed, but it is Rachel's 'conduct' (and Sergeant Cuff's misreading of it) which keeps that plot in motion. The mystery of the disappearance of the Diamond becomes submerged in the mystery of Rachel's conduct. In effect Rachel also goes missing – by means of her silence, her strangely altered behaviour to Franklin, her self-incarceration in her room and subsequent removal from her home, and by means of the hysteria which is represented as 'an absence of all ladylike restraint in her language and manner' (*M* 200). Rachel thus becomes the mystery, the puzzle to be solved, and the cherished object that is restored to its domestic setting after careful detective work.

In Rachel we encounter yet again that collocation of female assertiveness and hysteria which we saw in Magdalen Vanstone. Rachel's strange 'conduct...under a sudden emergency' is simply an extension of that 'defect' of 'secrecy and self-will' (*M* 53) which makes her 'odd and wild' (*M* 217), and marks her everyday conduct as different from other girls of her class and age.

> She was unlike most other girls of her age, in this – that she had ideas of her own, and was stiff-necked enough to set the fashions themselves at defiance, if the fashions did not suit her views. In trifles, this independence of hers was well enough; but in matters of importance, it carried her (as my lady thought, and as I thought)

too far. She judged for herself...never told you beforehand what she was going to do; never came with secrets and confidences ...[and] always went on a way of her own. (*M* 52–3, emphasis added)

Self-will, independence, ideas of her own, the desire to judge for herself, keeping her own counsel, disregard for convention – these markers of Rachel's distinctiveness from other girls are also the signs of Eliza Lynn Linton's 'Girl of the Period', that embodiment of mid-Victorian fears about the nature of modern femininity, who first appeared in the *Saturday Review* in 1868, the year in which *The Moonstone* was published.

Collins's representation of Rachel is deeply ambivalent. It is full of the contradictions that characterized nineteenth-century discourses on femininity, and especially those on feminine feeling. Although they are constantly perceived as 'odd' and 'wild' by her family and friends, Rachel's secrecy, her self-dependence and exceptional self-control are, in a sense only heightened versions of those virtues of self-containment, modesty and restraint which were universally recommended to respectable middle-class women, and were, indeed, the defining characteristics of the domestic feminine ideal. Rachel's real secret, however, is that her self-containment and self-control mask her fear of a fundamental lack of control, and an inability to contain her feelings, especially her feelings for Franklin Blake.

While the male characters work to detect the thief, Rachel is engaged in a psychic drama of detecting what she perceives as the awful truth about herself: that she cannot 'tear from [her] heart' her love for a man she knows (on the evidence of her own eyes) to be unworthy. This guilty secret is a peculiarly feminine one:

Oh, how can I find words to say it in! How can I make a *man* understand that a feeling which horrifies me at myself, can be a feeling that fascinates me at the same time? (*M* 233)

As is the case with most sensation heroines, the drama of Rachel's feelings and sensations is displayed as a spectacle to the reader, and is the source of some of the novel's most sensational writing. The climax of this drama occurs in Chapter 7 of 'The Discovery of the Truth', in which Rachel is in thrall to her feelings – at least as seen from the perspective of Franklin Blake, the narrator of this section. For most of this chapter she is represented as moving like an automaton, propelled by the messages of the body, mesmerized by the sound of Franklin's voice, and mastered by his touch. The result is an orgy of hysterical self-abasement:

> 'I am worse, if worse can be, than you are yourself.' Sobs and tears burst from her. She struggled with them fiercely...'I can't tear you out of my heart...even now! You may trust in the shameful, shameful weakness which can only struggle against you in this way!...O God! I despise myself even more heartily than I despise *him!'* (M 350)

This chapter plays on the readers' contradictory fears and desires about femininity. It displays the spectacle of the exquisite anguish of Rachel's 'illicit' passion for a man whom she 'knows' to be unworthy of the love of a respectable woman, for the delight of a reader who knows that the man in the case is honourable.

Another version of the spectacle of female passion is found in the letter in which Rosanna Spearman declares her love for Franklin Blake. In Rosanna's case, as in Rachel's, a woman's passion is associated with secrecy and silence, but it is given a different class inflection. Rachel, a representative (however disordered) of genteel femininity, retreats into silence in order to protect the reputation of the man she loves – and perhaps also because she does not wish to expose her own guilt in having loved an apparent criminal. The respectability of middle-class masculinity is thus preserved by the self-sacrificing silence of a colluding woman. On the other hand, the servant Rosanna sees her silence as a direct form of power, and a potential means of closing the class gap. The reward for Rachel's collusion is marriage, the price of Rosanna's delusion is self-destruction.

The intersections of class and gender are particularly important in the novel's central plot situation, the crisis in the family and household. The nineteenth-century household was defined as a predominantly feminine space and the ideals of femininity and of domesticity were each defined in terms of the other. However, if the woman, as wife and mother, was the queen of the domestic domain and keeper of the household temple, the home and household were also the means of containing and controlling both women and those feared aspects of femininity that were suppressed by the domestic ideal. *The Moonstone* calls attention to the family's role in policing femininity by its use of Sergeant Cuff, the family policeman, who, 'for the last twenty years...[has] been largely employed in cases of family scandal, acting in the capacity of confidential man' (*M* 163). Cuff's role (and it is one he quite self-consciously pursues) is to seek out the criminal secrets of the family, and to contain them 'within the family limits' (*M* 166). As this outsider informs the insider Betteredge, 'I have put the muzzle on worse family difficulties than this in my time' (*M* 132). Cuff's success derives largely from his practice of getting the family to police itself: 'The less noise made, and the fewer strangers employed...the better' (*M* 166). The evidence of Cuff's 'domestic practice' (*M* 163) and the assumption on which it is based is that the family is a prime site of criminality. However, his genteel clients project the dis-ease of the family onto the detective, as in Lady Verinder's 'presentiment that he is bringing trouble and misery with him into the house' (*M* 105). For nineteenth-century readers the sensation plot itself was, very often, a way of displacing various kinds of uneasiness about the dis-ease of the family.

Cuff's flawed expertise as the policeman of the family plays a vital part in keeping the mystery narrative in process. Cuff is defeated by the silence of women (Rachel and Rosanna), by feminine reticence (Lady Verinder), and the failure of individual women to conform to dominant stereotypes of femininity. Cuff retires from the fray having correctly concluded that Rachel is the key to the mystery, but having falsely diagnosed the nature of the mystery. His misdiagnosis is the result of his over-confidence in the lessons of his 'domestic practice', which leads to his misreading of the signs of Rachel Verinder's conduct. His mistake is to subsume the particular woman into the generality 'Woman', and to assume that all 'young ladies of rank and position' (*M* 164) are the same.

Despite his experience of the family and young ladies, Cuff is wrong-footed because, as a lower-class man, he is unable, finally, to understand the upper-middle-class family and the genteel femininity upon which it is predicated. Cuff and, for that matter, the Verinder family lawyer Bruff, huff and puff good-naturedly but leaden-footedly around the subject of woman, unable to fathom her mysteries. Cuff and Bruff are the comic side of *The Moonstone's* preoccupation (a common preoccupation in the sensation novel) with the problematic relationship of men to the feminine space of the affective family – as opposed to the family as legal, economic entity.

The manner in which Franklin Blake and Godfrey Ablewhite are depicted, and their roles in the sensation plot also throw interesting light on the sensation novel's concern with men, masculinity and the family. The blurring of gender categories that is evident in the feminized lower-middle-class artist Hartright, and the hystericized (and hence feminized) *déclassé* Ozias Midwinter, are also seen in Blake and Ablewhite. Ablewhite, as it turns out, is a ladies' man in the usually accepted sense, but for most of the novel he is portrayed as quite a different kind of ladies' man. This smooth-shaven man with his 'head of lovely long flaxen hair, falling negligently over the poll of his neck' (*M* 54) has thoroughly penetrated the world of female philanthropy, and serves as the lone male on all its committees. Franklin Blake's ambivalent gender status, on the other hand, is connected with his unconventional (i.e. not English public school) and dilettante foreign education, and his lack of a clearly defined social role. The son of a wealthy man who aspires to a dukedom, he pursues a somewhat outdated aristocratic mode of living and has no professional training or vocation. He is one of several sensation heroes who indulge a taste for French novels and German philosophy while waiting to come into their father's money. 'He wrote a little; he painted a little; he sang and composed a little' (*M* 15) whilst leading a nomadic existence and borrowing and giving money in a 'lively, easy way' (*M* 15).

Although feminine passion and the mystery of feminine silence are the main forces which keep this sensation narrative in process, it is these two feminized males who start it off: Franklin has the role of 'messenger', since it is he who brings the Diamond into the house, and Franklin and Godfrey both play a part in its disappearance. In Franklin's case the disappearance of the Diamond is the first stage in the process by which he becomes fully socialized and masculinized. He becomes caught up in the pervasive 'detective fever' occasioned by the

Diamond's disappearance, but his search for its thief is but a means to another end. It is, in fact, a quest: it is both a task he sets himself, in the manner of the romance hero, to prove himself worthy of his lady's love, and a quest to fathom the mystery of his lady, 'to find out the secret of her silence towards her mother, and her enmity towards *me*' (M 291). Blake's quest also turns out to be a quest for identity, both his own and Rachel's. His detective work produces a crisis of personal identity. It also involves him in plumbing the depths of his own and Rachel's unconscious, when he submits to replaying the events of the night of the Diamond's disappearance, and when he acts as a kind of psychoanalyst to Rachel, compelling her to tell the story of what she saw in the bedroom – a kind of primal scene. The end of the quest, and the resolution of the mystery is not, as one might have expected, the discovery of the Diamond. Rather it is the discovery of the 'true' identities of Franklin and Rachel as the renovators of the family through romantic love and companionate marriage.

The final destination of this narrative, like all sensation novels (indeed like most mid-Victorian novels) is marriage. However, the end of the *narration* serves to reinsert this romantic marriage into the complex context of Victorian sexual customs. The ending of *The Moonstone* foregrounds the way in which respectable Victorian marriage and genteel femininity were defined in terms of, and indeed constructed in relation to, prostitution and fallen women. When we read the cynically narrated story of Ablewhite's domestic arrangements and his secret life in the suburbs (and it is interesting to note that it is Sergeant Cuff, the policeman of the respectable family, who is the cynical narrator here), we may perhaps be led to the conclusion that the real disrupter of 'our quiet English house' was not the Diamond, but a fallen woman – the kept 'lady in the villa', 'such familiar objects in London life' (M 448).

DOING THE POLICE IN DIFFERENT VOICES

The narrative structure and methods of narration of sensation novels are organized around concealment and the prolongation of mystery and suspense in a kind of 'narrative hide-and-seek'.[19]

In his sensation novels, Collins pursued this game of narrative hide-and-seek by means of multiple narrators, or by the creation of multiple-narrator effects through the use of letters, journals and other documents. This use of multiple narrators with their linked and overlapping narratives creates an impression of verisimilitude or actuality. It also permits a range of different voices to be heard, speaking from different social and gender perspectives. Servants and lower-class characters add their voices and stories to those of their masters, mistresses and other social superiors. Women's voices are heard, sometimes talking to themselves in diaries and journals, and sometimes talking to other women in letters. The documents and personal accounts that make up Collins's narratives are forms of testimony, which sometimes read like the evidence of witnesses in a court of law, or the 'I was there' school of journalism. They are also used to give a privileged access to a character's interiority.

However, although the individual narratives have the authority that comes from direct observation and experience, and bear many of the marks of realism, it is not the totalizing realism that we tend to associate with the mid-Victorian novel. The separate narratives are not only individual, they are also quite clearly idiosyncratic, subjective, quirky and partial. They are also limited; each particular narrator only knows part of the story, or, as in the case of *The Woman in White* and *The Moonstone*, is under strict instructions to confine him- or herself to what he or she actually experienced. The result is a fragmentation of narrative and a dispersal of narrative authority. Instead of the utterance of the sagacious, omniscient narrator of the realist novel, we have a heap of fragments, linked either by the invisible hand of the impersonal narrator in *No Name* and *Armadale*, or by the editorializing of Hartright in *The Woman in White* and Blake in *The Moonstone*. In the last two cases there *is* a kind of totalizing vision, but its imperative is subjective – the desire of the hero/detective/narrator to assert his mastery over experience and events by making them tell his story: a story of rationality, causality and control.

These aspects of the sensation narrative may be seen as symptomatic of a crisis of narrative authority in the mid-nineteenth-century novel, and also of wider cultural develop-ments. The fragmentation of the narrative voice, and/or the

58

unreliability of the third-person narrator in Collins's novels (and perhaps in sensation fiction more generally), is related to what Raymond Williams has called the disappearance of the 'knowable community'.[20] The fiction of the earlier part of the nineteenth century represented a world that was presumed to be 'knowable', which could be held together and comprehended by a single consciousness. For example, Jane Austen with her 'two or three families in a country village' preserved the fiction of a community which could still be known and possessed by an omniscient narrator. The growth of cities, an increasing social complexity, and changing ways of conceptualizing social existence challenged this totalizing view. Dickens's or Collins's London could not be comprehended in the same way as Austen's Bath.

In Collins's novels the narrator cedes authority to the detective – most frequently to the amateur detective who is also a central actor in the mystery whose story is being told. The 'detective' teases out the story that the narrator cannot or will not tell. Facts, events and connections are uncovered or recovered until the knowledge of the reader and the detective(s) coalesces. Far from being the reader's guide and friend, sensation narrators cannot be entirely trusted. They litter our path with false clues, and leave us to make provisional (often wrong) judgements. They allow us temporarily to sympathize with characters and predicaments which both the plot and conventional morality ultimately require us to reject. Thus moral relativism creeps in, at least until the final denouement, and even then it does not always entirely disappear. The reader's sensation of being misled, or temporarily abandoned, by the narrator – of being left free to witness directly the thoughts and actions of unconventional, socially or sexually transgressive or morally dubious characters without the intervention of an all-seeing, all-knowing narrator – is one of the thrills of Collins's sensation novels.

COLLINS AND SENSATIONALISM BEYOND THE 1860s

For much of the twentieth century critics tended to share the nineteenth-century reviewers' view that Collins's sensation novels of the 1860s were the peak of his achievement, and that his fiction lost its power after *The Moonstone*.[21] In the 1870s and 1880s, it was argued, Collins's sensationalism was overpowered by his 'mission'. In fact, from *Basil* onwards, Collins had always been a novelist with a mission, and his sensation fictions of the 1860s all engaged critically with a range of contemporary social issues. Moreover, although his subject matter changed after the 1860s and he often struggled to keep pace with changing fictional tastes and to make sense of a changing literary marketplace, Collins continued to deploy the ingredients of the sensation novel and his talent as 'an ingenious storyteller'.[22] To a great extent, complicated plots involving murder, madness, bigamy, adultery, divorce, desertion, fraud, deception and blackmail remained his stock in trade. So did melodrama, Gothic, mystery and detection, although in the later novels these were sometimes exaggerated (almost to the point of self-parody) and combined in a rather awkward manner rather than in the confidently playful mode of his earlier fictions. This section outlines the persistence of sensational themes and devices in a selection of the baker's dozen of novels which Collins published after *The Moonstone*.

Man and Wife (1870) is often cited as Collins's first didactic work. The author clearly invites this view of the novel in his Preface which announces that this 'fiction is founded on facts, and aspires to afford what help it may towards hastening the reform of certain abuses which have been too long suffered to exist among us unchecked' (*M&W* 5). The novel is an attack on 'the present scandalous condition of the Marriage Laws of the United Kingdom' and on the restricted legal and property rights of married women, as Collins explained in the Preface which he wrote just as the 1870 Married Women's Property Bill was about to be enacted. 'The Story' of the novel, which is organized in fifteen scenes, arises from the inconsistencies both within and between the Irish, Scottish and English marriage laws. In 'A Prologue' set in 1855, which precedes 'The Story', an English lawyer exploits a loophole in the Irish marriage laws that enables a client to annul his marriage in order to further his social and political career. In the main narrative, set some dozen years later, the client's daughter, Anne, is seduced and abandoned by the lawyer's son, Geoffrey Delamayn, who having first sought to manipulate the Scottish custom and practice of irregular marriage to his own advantage is then trapped by them in a marriage to Anne. In demonstrating the iniquities of the current state of the marriage laws, Collins deploys an extremely complicated plot and combines sensation, melodrama, domestic Gothic, the incarceration of a wronged wife, an actual murder, a murder plot, the blackmail of a woman with a secret, madness, and the ghosts conjured by a madwoman's guilt. The murderous madwoman is Hester Dethridge whose mind has been unhinged by her crime and the suffering which led to it. Her secret is revealed when Geoffrey discovers a manuscript in which she confesses to the murder (many years ago) of the drunken husband who had repeatedly mistreated and robbed her of her earnings and possessions, all with the full sanction of the law. Geoffrey seeks to use the confession to blackmail Hester into helping him murder Anne, using the same ingenious method by which she had despatched her husband without attracting suspicion to herself. Hester, however, is distracted by the apparition which periodically torments her and instead turns her attack on Geoffrey. The novel ends, as many sensation novels do, with the confinement of a transgressive woman (Hester) in an asylum and the restitution of Anne's social status and fortunes through marriage to a kindly and wealthy older man.

The story of Mercy Merrick, a prostitute who tries to reform herself under the influence of the charismatic radical preacher Julian Gray, *The New Magdalen* (1873) certainly tackled a sensational subject as well as recycling some of the plot elements of Collins's earlier sensation novels. For example, Mercy commits identity theft when she takes on the identity of Grace Rosebury whom she believes to have been killed when they are working as volunteer nurses in the Franco-German war of 1870. In this case this identity-swap reverses the usual sensation novel formula by making the impostor, rather than the person whose identity is stolen, the object of the reader's sympathy. Returning to England, Mercy/Grace takes on a new social identity as the companion of Grace's relative, Lady Roy, and also as the fiancée of a successful journalist. Mercy's new social position is threatened and her moral capacity tested when Grace, who has recovered from her injuries, returns to England and seeks to assert her claim to her true identity. In another reversal of the sensation fiction formula the sympathetically portrayed Mercy is cast in the role of a villainess as she maintains her deception, while the unsympathetic Grace is cast in the role of victim. There is some suspense as to whether Mercy will continue to maintain her assumed identity and it is only when Grace is threatened with incarceration in an asylum, on the grounds that she is suffering from an insane delusion, that Mercy confesses to her deception. Mercy's confession, which is also prompted by her acceptance of Julian's version of her, results in the union of the former prostitute and the priest, and their search for a new authentic identity in the New World.

The Law and the Lady (1875) returns to the detective story format. Its heroine, Valeria Brinton, a determined and resourceful woman of the Marian Halcombe type, seeks to defend her marriage by becoming what her uncle describes as a 'lawyer[s] in petticoats' (*L&L* 21). Valeria takes on the role of detective when she discovers that her husband's oddly secretive behaviour derives from his experience of being tried for the murder of his first wife and receiving a verdict of 'Not Proven'. As she pursues her quest to overturn this verdict against Eustace Macallen Valeria both consciously and unconsciously adopts a range of roles and identities. She consciously adopts the guise of what she assumes to be Major Fitz-David's idea of femininity when she seeks information from this aging rake, but is surprised by the way in which this role playing blurs her sense of herself: 'I seemed in some way to have lost my ordinary identity' (*L&L* 7). As her quest proceeds both Valeria and the reader are faced with questions about her identity and her motivations: 'What do we know of our own lives?' she asks at the novel's conclusion, 'What do we know of the fulfilment of our dearest wishes?' (*L&L* 413). Valeria's narrative contains an embedded sensation novel, in the form of the transcript of Macallen's original trial which she reads in the course of her investigation. Like *The Woman in White* and *The Moonstone*, this transcript is made up of various testimonies and extracts from journals which conceal as much as they reveal. However, perhaps the most sensational feature of *The Law and the Lady* is the bizarre character of Miserrimus Dexter, a wildly extravagant reworking of Henry Fairlie, the degenerate aesthete from *The*

Woman in White. With 'the eyes and hands of a beautiful woman' and a body which, although lacking legs, is of 'manly proportions', Dexter is 'literally the half of a man' (*L&L* 73). Feminized by his nerves and his propensity to hysteria, and at the same time, sadistic, aggressive and sexually predatory, he is a grotesque hybrid. 'This most multiform of living beings' (*L&L* 44) challenges the idea of single unified identity and also calls into question what it means to be a man.

In 1878 Collins followed Mary Elizabeth Braddon's example and signed up with Tillotson's fiction bureau for the syndicated publication of a novel that recycled the plot of his 1858 play *The Red Vial*. *Jezebel's Daughter* retains the outline and detail of the play's simple melodrama of murder and madness but reframes them by having the events of the late 1820s narrated from the perspective of 1878. Using a sensational plot involving poisonings, plottings around a marriage, theft, and a sensational scene in the Deadhouse, the novel contrasts the very different ways in which two widows appropriate and apply their husbands' power. The good widow, Mrs Wagner, takes up the legacy of her husband's reforming liberalism by employing fallen women as clerks in a business which she successfully manages, and by rescuing Jack Straw from an old-fashioned lunatic asylum and using Samuel Tuke's modern methods of moral management to care for him. The bad widow, Madame Fontaine, is revealed as the cause of Straw's apparent 'lunacy', which has in fact been caused when she used him as a human subject in her attempts to appropriate her husband's scientific power by experimenting with the collection of poisons and antidotes which he had ordered to be destroyed on his death. The woman who meddles in science is explored further in *Heart and Science* (1883) which uses a sensation plot to attack vivisection and the dehumanizing tendencies of modern science and to explore a range of degenerative modern types. The sensation plot involves the attempts of Mrs Gallilee (an active member of numerous scientific committees) to retain access to the inheritance of her nervously susceptible ward, Carmina Graywell, by thwarting her union with Ovid Vere, her son from her first marriage – and the novel's good scientist. Succumbing to a nervous shock brought about by Mrs Gallilee's false claim that she was illegitimate, Carmina is incompetently treated by the Gallilee's family doctor and observed with detached scientific curiosity by Mrs Gallilee's friend, Dr Nathan Benjulia, a specialist in brain diseases and nervous disorders (and a rumoured vivisectionist), before being rescued from the brink of death by Ovid who returns from his self-imposed exile in Canada to treat her with a new method which he has encountered there. Mrs Gallilee is threatened with incarceration in an asylum, but escapes the fate that in an earlier sensation novel might well have been her due punishment. Instead she recovers from the nervous breakdown induced by her failed plotting and returns to her self-enclosed life of scientific committees, oblivious of the damage she has done and the extent of her alienation from her family.

Collins's last completed novel, *The Legacy of Cain* (1888), and the posthumously published *Blind Love* (1890) which was completed by Walter Besant (on Collins's instructions) have both been described as 'exercises in old-fashioned sensationalism'.[23] *The Legacy of Cain* certainly returns to some of the character types, plot elements and devices of Collins's sensation novels of the 1860s, including: women with a secret, murderous mad women, female criminality, inter-generational discord and inherited characteristics. However, in this novel these sensation elements are deployed in a speculative fiction which engages with the post-Darwinian debates about the inheritance and transmission of degenerate conditions, criminality and insanity which had become so influential by the late 1880s. These debates are dramatized in the 'First Period' of the novel, set in a prison, in which a doctor, a clergyman and a prison governor discuss the moral and medical issues raised by the case of a prisoner recently sentenced to death for the brutal murder of her husband. Rejecting the doctor's degenerationist view that vices and diseases are more likely to descend to children than virtue and health, the Reverend Abel Gracedieu seeks to demonstrate his belief in the influence of environment and the shaping power of upbringing and moral management by bringing up the murderess's infant daughter alongside his own, without revealing which is his natural child. The stories of these two girls are recovered and reconstructed by the prison governor and through the juxtaposition of their diaries which give the reader privileged access to their consciousness. The recovered events and the diaries reveal that the vicar's natural daughter has inherited her mother's latent 'moral insanity', which is manifested in her own self-obsession and ultimately in her plan to murder her husband. The murderess's daughter on the other hand is revealed as combining the innocent, trusting, passivity of the feminine ideal with a kind of unconscious awareness of her mother's criminality. The former renders her incapable of resisting her adoptive sister's stealing of her suitor. The latter is manifested in trances in which she assumes a violent second self, but whose promptings she is able ultimately to master because of the soundness of her upbringing.

In his final novel, *Blind Love*, Collins returned to the conventional sensation tale of a headstrong girl, Iris Henley, who marries an unsuitable man, Lord Harry Norland, in opposition to her father's wishes. However, he updated this plot situation by making the unsuitable man a member of the Invincibles – a splinter group of the Irish Republican Brotherhood which was active in Dublin in the 1880s and which was involved in the Phoenix Park Murders in 1882. Like many sensation novels *Blind Love* has at its centre a white collar crime, a domestic incarceration, and an identity substitution: in this case the crime is an insurance fraud which involves luring Oxbye, a consumptive patient, to Harry's home to await death and then claiming that the dead man is Harry. When the dying patient who was selected for his close physical resemblance to Harry begins to recover, he is poisoned by Harry's accomplice in a scene which is secretly observed (in true sensation novel fashion) by Iris's maid Fanny. Iris later exposes the fraud when a letter from Fanny informs her that the consumptive patient did not die of natural causes. As in so many sensation novels the perpetrators of this crime are dealt with by extra-legal devices: Iris pays back her share of the proceeds and Harry agrees to do the same if no further action is taken against her; Harry's accomplice, Vimpany, drowns. Perhaps most intriguingly, Collins concludes his final novel as he did his first major success, *The Woman in White*, by using rivalries within a secret political society as the means of punishing a plotter. However, in this case there is also an element of gentlemanly self-sacrifice, as Harry travels openly to Ireland in the full knowledge that he will be killed by the Invincibles.

3

The Women's Sensation Novel

Sensation became the rage, and sensations were demanded every hour.... [S]peedily a phalanx of lady-novelists sprang up...armed with the 'Newgate Calendar,' the Annals of the Divorce Court, the gossip of the smoking-room, the *argot* of the race-course...[I]n the pages of sensation novels, especially in those which are penned by the gentler sex, vice runs riot, and crime reigns supreme...[It] is curious that Society should not only permit such a monstrous libel on its own character, but should also complacently reward its libellers.[1]

This is the age of the lady novelists, and lady novelists naturally give first place to the heroine[s]...[who are] pictured as high-strung women, full of passion, purpose, and movement – very liable to error. Now the most interesting side of a woman's character is her relation to the other sex, and the errors of women that are most interesting spring out of this relation.[2]

[N]ovels in which woman plays a...much more exciting part... [now] ride in triumph. If, as French sociologists are never tired of telling us, woman in a special manner reflects her surroundings, it is only natural that the clever ladies who supply our circulating libraries should reflect in their writings the change in the spirit and taste of the age, and go to Bow Street and the Divorce Court for their inspirations.[3]

Women played an extremely important part in putting sensation, in all its various meanings and forms, into the sensation novel. Indeed, for many contemporary commentators one of the most sensational (and deplorable) things about the sensation genre was the prominence of women writers. In his satire on the novels of Braddon and Wood, *Lucretia: or the Heroine of the Nineteenth Century* (1868), the Reverend Francis E. Paget declared:

No *man* would have dared to write and publish such books...no *man could* have written such delineations of female passion...No! They are women, who by their writings have been doing the work of the enemy of souls, glossing over vice, making profligacy attractive, detailing with licentious minuteness the workings of unbridled passions, encouraging vanity, extravagance, wilfulness, selfishness...Women have done this, – have thus abused their power and prostituted their gifts; – who might have been bright and shining lights in their generation.[4]

Sensation novels were, in the main (or so it was thought), written by wicked women, about wayward girls and wicked women, for consumption by women whose waywardness and potential for wickedness was signalled by the very fact that they read such material. This unhealthy relationship between women writers, readers and fictional subjects was castigated by Margaret Oliphant, who conducted a one-woman campaign against the genre (although, with her accustomed shrewd professional eye, she also saw that sensationalism played a major part in energizing the rather tame domestic novel, and increasing the market for fiction).

It is a shame to women so to write; and it is a shame to the women who read and accept as a true representation of themselves and their ways the equivocal talk and fleshly inclinations herein attributed to them. Their patronage of such books is in reality an adoption and acceptance of them.[5]

The feminine note in sensation fiction was not, however, simply a question of female authorship. The sensation novel was perceived as a feminine phenomenon regardless of the gender of the particular sensation writer. It was yet another symptom of the creeping feminization of literature and culture which began with Samuel Richardson and the sentimental novel in the eighteenth century, and became more pronounced (and more hysterically denounced) as the nineteenth century went on.[6] It is interesting to note that while the sensation novel was making its stir, writers, readers and critics of poetry were also heatedly debating the Fleshly School of Poetry. Like the sensation novel, the poetry of the Fleshly School – which included poems by Dante Gabriel Rossetti, A. C. Swinburne, George Meredith and others – was full of bold and sensual images of 'fallen' and other women, and dealt powerfully with physical sensations. The debate about these poems, like the debate about the sensation novel, turned on issues of gender and ideas about the nature of femininity: the advocates of fleshly poetry declaring that dominant ideas of feminine purity should not be allowed to constrain (masculine) art, and its critics countering that the mode of representation employed – a riot of sensual detail as Alfred Austin put it in his 1869 essay on Swinburne in *Temple Bar*[7] – constituted a feminization or even an effeminization of art.

The production and consumption of sensation fiction, and its contemporary critical reception were closely linked, not only to general ideas about 'the feminine', but also to various aspects of the Woman Question: to debates about women's legal and political rights, women's educational and employment aspirations and opportunities, and women's dissatisfactions with and resistance to traditional marital and familial patterns. For instance, a review of Braddon's fiction in the *New Review* (1863) explicitly linked the strong, independent sensation heroine to current debates on the position of women:

> When we hear…so much about employment for young women, and so much scorn cast upon the old-fashioned theory, according to which they are intended as help-meets for man…are we not driven to ask ourselves whether woman's character is of a kind to *bear* emancipation from male control and influence?[8]

The critical recovery and re-vision of the sensation novel in the latter third of the twentieth century was also linked to the Woman Question. The re-reading of the women's sensation novel was, for the most part, undertaken by feminist critics and literary and cultural historians pursuing their interests in women as writers, readers and written. The women's sensation novel was thus relocated in cultural history by a feminist scholarship that contextualized and historicized the processes of canon-formation, and looked more closely at the various ways in which women's writing has been used to construct the boundary between popular and high art. In particular, feminist critics and cultural historians in the latter part of the twentieth century re-examined the evaluative system by means of which generations of students had been taught 'to equate popularity with debasement, emotionality with ineffectiveness…domesticity with triviality, and all of these, implicitly, with womanly inferiority'.[9]

Other important new perspectives on the women's sensation novel were provided by feminist work on modern mass-culture forms such as the romantic novel and soap opera. For example, Tania Modleski's *Loving With a Vengeance* (1984) offered a suggestive analysis of the semiotics of the popular romance text and the cultural meaning and significance of genre, discovering 'elements of protest and resistance underneath highly "ortho-dox" plots'.[10] Modleski rethought the relationships between current 'mass market fantasies for women' and the women's genres of the past, and analysed them in terms of the complex and contradictory pleasures which they offer to both women readers and women writers. Her analysis of Gothic and other women's genres of the eighteenth and early-nineteenth centuries offered a useful model for re-reading the women's sensation novel which, like Gothic, reworks the conventions and assumptions of the domestic novel – 'driving home to women the importance of coping with enforced confinement and the paranoid fear it generates'.[11]

Other feminist work on the texts of modern popular romance interrogated the metaphors of passivity, appetite and consumption which had hitherto dominated thinking about the way in which women in particular receive the texts of popular culture. For example, Janice Radway's[12] influential work on Harlequin romance (the American equivalent of Mills and Boon) and its readers combined ethnographic analysis of actual romance readers and reading communities, with reader-response theory and feminist psychoanalysis to produce a view of the activity of romance reading as a deeply contradictory experience; women readers, paradoxically, appear to immerse themselves in narratives which make an idealized version of domesticity an object of desire, in order to resist and escape, at least temporarily, the limitations of their own domestic and familial roles. Radway's work, like that of Alison Light, and Bridget Fowler,[13] led to a reassessment of the conventional view that popular romance forms for women depend on the reader's simple identification with the romantic heroine. On the contrary, romance texts offer their readers a range of identifica-tions and positions, which readers quite commonly negotiate in complex ways, reading against the grain of the (frequently) conservative ideology of the formulaic romance text.

Late twentieth-century work on other modern mass-culture narrative forms also offered new ways of reading the popular texts of the nineteenth century: for example, the so-called 'woman's film' (usually a weepy melodrama) and television soap opera. Work on the 'male gaze', on the ways in which the visual text addresses and positions its readers, and the kinds of gendered subjectivity it constructs for them was usefully appropriated for a re-reading of the women's sensation novel. For example, the feminist intervention in the 'largely negative accounts of female spectatorship, suggesting colonized, alienated or masochistic positions of identification',[14] was particularly useful for re-examining what is at issue in the sensation novel's invitation to its female readers to identify with or to spectate women who are victims, subjected to intense suffering, or punished for transgressive behaviour. Clearly care is needed; the print culture in which the sensation novel was produced was very different from the multimedia, mass culture in which radio and television soap opera, the film melodrama and modern mass-market romance fiction developed. Nevertheless the study of nineteenth-century literature and culture has gained much from engaging with the methodological and theoretical debates within modern cultural studies.

Another source of the renewed interest in the women's sensation novel in the late twentieth century – and this also overlaps interestingly with the nineteenth-century sensation controversy – was an interest in writing the *feminine* and the feminine in writing. Many of the contemporary anxieties about sensation fiction (especially, but not exclusively, as practised by women writers) were expressed as concerns about the 'feminine' nature of the writing itself. Nineteenth-century reviewers repeatedly complained that sensation fiction was written in a language of excess: it was extravagant, ornate, embellished; it knew no bounds (or if it did it wilfully ignored them); it dwelt long, lovingly and lavishly on descriptions of the body and of physical sensations – especially, it was objected, when the body or the feelings were those of a woman. Curiously, the reviewers in the middle-class magazines of the 1860s were just as concerned with *écriture féminine* and with writing the (female) body as were their late-twentieth-century successors. Needless to say, the disciples of Cixous and Irigaray viewed the matter differently and some sought to appropriate the women's sensation novel as a celebration of female power and feeling, a form of feminine writing which inscribed the body and feminine subjectivity. This was an interesting move, but it risked reinscribing essentialist ideas of the feminine and replicating the gendered critical discourse of the nineteenth century; the main difference was that twentieth-century feminist critics gave a positive valuation to the 'femininity' which was devalued and marginalized by their nineteenth-century predecessors.

THE SENSATIONAL SPECTACLE OF WOMAN

> There is no good end attained by trying to persuade ourselves that women are all incorporeal, angelic, colourless, passionless, helpless creatures...Women have especial need, as the world goes, to be shrewd, self-reliant, and strong; and we do all we can in our literature to render them helpless, imbecilic, and idiotic.[15]

If the sensation novel (and particularly the women's sensation novel) produced a moral panic among Victorian reviewers and cultural commentators, it was itself produced by another kind of panic – a panic about the nature of the feminine. By the 1860s, woman, womanhood and womanliness had all became contested terms, as had the institutions of marriage and the family around which these terms were constructed. The period of the sensation novel's greatest prominence was the decade which immediately followed the campaigns and debates leading up to the Divorce Act of 1857 (the Matrimonial Causes Act), the press campaigns on the 'social evil' of prostitution (which also reached a high point in 1857), and the 'surplus women' controversy and the associated campaigns for educational and employment opportunities for women. Throughout the 1860s, in increasingly strident tones, the newspaper and the periodical press made a spectacle of what they tended to call 'Woman', putting women or 'Woman' on display, and devoting increasing amounts of space to articles on the 'New Woman', the 'fast woman', or, most famously, the 'Girl of the Period'. Whatever the label, modern woman was uniformly portrayed as being in flight from motherhood, family responsibility and domestic existence. In

71

these articles, and especially in Eliza Lynn Linton's essay on 'The Girl of the Period' (first published in the *Saturday Review*, 14 March 1868), femininity itself was put under the spotlight as an inherently problematic state involving duplicity and potentially uncontrollable feeling, and women were variously represented as primitives, savages, hysterics and whores. The women's sensation novel was part of this developing discourse on the modern woman: it was both a response to and part of social change and a changing conceptualization of women. It also became part of the evidence of these changes.

Above all the women's sensation novel seemed to be concerned with a new sense of marriage and the family as problematic institutions for both women and men. Marriage, the resolution of life's trials and the desired goal of romantic and domestic fiction, is, on the contrary, the source of many of life's trials in the sensation novel. The main focus is on the predicament of women, but masculine perspectives on the family and their troubled experience of romantic love and marriage are also examined in some detail. The novels of Braddon and Wood, for example, are peopled by frustrated, independent, even mad and murderous women, troubled and troubling wives and mothers, as well as by betrayed and betraying husbands, who are either bored or boring, and almost always fail to understand their wives and the domestic sphere in general. Strained relations between parents and children, and tensions between siblings are another common feature of these novels.

The sensation novel's preoccupation with marriage questions was frequently articulated in the form of the bigamy plot. Indeed, so common was the female sensationalists' use of this plot that the 'bigamy novel' came to be regarded as a subgenre of the sensation novel. Geraldine Jewsbury, who as a publisher's reader had to wade through numerous manuscripts of derivative bigamy novels, gave vent to her spleen on the genre in a rather illuminating *Athenaeum* review of John Berwick Harwood's *Lord Lynn's Wife*, a novel she had recommended for rejection.

> If, in after-times the manners and customs of English life in 1864 were to be judged from the novels of the day, it would naturally be believed that people, in the best regulated families, were in the habit of marrying two wives, or two husbands...and of suppressing the

one that proved inconvenient, either by 'painless extinction' or by more forcible methods.[16]

This is a salutary warning on the use of literature as 'evidence' of social trends. Nevertheless, the novels of 1864 do, in fact, give the reader of 'after-times' much valuable evidence about the concerns and anxieties, if not the practices of the best-regulated families of the Victorian bourgeoisie. Jewsbury also offers a perceptive analysis of the socio-legal origins and psychological appeal of the bigamy plot.

> Heroes and heroines of the present generation of novels rarely dispense with the marriage ceremony altogether, – it would be a want of propriety which would shock both author and reader; but illegal marriage and supernumerary ceremonies are the order of the day...[and] we must conclude that there is a great deal of latent sympathy with this state of things, which an author can appeal to with the certainty of exciting the reader's lively interest.[17]

Bigamy in the sensation novel is often, perhaps, almost always, accidental or inadvertent; that is to say it involves a marriage which both of the partners believe to be valid, but which is not – usually because of some legal oddity or the erroneous belief that the first husband or wife is dead. This kind of bigamy plot had a powerful psychological appeal for contemporary readers, and was a useful narrative device in the respectable middle-class novel – and this, for all its flirtations with the risqué, is what the sensation novel remained. Such plots involve moral complexity as well as narrative complication. As Jeanne Fahnestock pointed out in her excellent essay on the subject, inadvertent or unintentional bigamy plots 'allow their protagonists to be paradoxically both innocent and guilty at the same time'.[18] They offer the chance 'to sin and be innocent...to see unsocial desires fulfilled and duly punished'. These plots also allow readers to identify with an apparently sexually transgressive and guilty character, and vicariously to experience a guilt from which they are subsequently released – a very satisfying process.

French novels have adultery; the English, more concerned with propriety and the blush on the cheek of the young person, stick to bigamy. True, on the whole. But, of course, one must remember the interesting exception. *East Lynne*, written by the conservative Ellen Wood, and one of the most popular novels of the nineteenth century, is a novel whose nobly suffering heroine is incontrovertibly an adulteress. However, even in this case (perhaps, as we shall see later, *especially* in this case), the bigamy convention is kept in play. Although Carlyle, the 'betrayed' husband who divorces his wife, does not remarry until he has good reason to believe his first wife is dead, he nevertheless suspects himself of being a bigamist when he discovers that the governess employed by his new wife is, in fact, his first (divorced) wife in disguise: 'the first thought that came thumping through his brain was, that he must be a man of two wives' (*EL* 614). Carlyle's reaction dramatizes a new moral experience created by the reformed divorce laws: a tension between marriage merely as a socio-legal arrangement on the one hand, and moral and religious conceptions of marriage on the other. Some sensation novelists developed what one might call spiritual or imagined bigamy or adultery plots, in which heroines who are legally married to one man feel themselves to be spiritually or emotionally married to another, or, alternatively, in which single heroines feel themselves to be bound to unattainable or married men. Rhoda Broughton's *Cometh Up As A Flower* and *Not Wisely But Too Well*, which are discussed in the final section of this chapter, are good examples of this species of what Oliphant described as 'innocent indecency'.[19]

An adulterous or bigamous marriage would, of course, be a fairly substantial skeleton to have in the family cupboard. As noted in the previous chapter, family secrets, and fundamental fears about the nature and structure of the family were central to Collins's novels. Such fearful secrets were, perhaps, even more important in the women's sensation novel. Indeed Elaine Showalter, writing mainly on the female sensationalists, argued that 'the power of Victorian sensation derives...from its exposure of secrecy as the fundamental and enabling condition of middle-class life'.[20] The sensationalists' obsession with family secrets was certainly much remarked upon by their first readers. In 'Sensation Novelists: Miss Braddon', W. Fraser Rae (quoting the Archbishop of York) protested that novelists like Braddon:

> want to persuade people that in almost every one of the well-ordered houses of their neighbours there was a skeleton shut up in some cupboard; that their comfortable and easy-looking neighbour

had in his breast a secret story which he was always going about trying to conceal.[21]

This persuasion is by no means a hidden subtext of the women's sensation novel; it is very much part of the textual surface. Characters speculate about 'the mysteries that may hang about the houses we enter' and 'foul deeds...done under the most hospitable roofs (*LAS* 140). The omniscient narrators of Braddon and Wood opine that 'few of us are without some secret skeleton that we have to keep from the world' (Wood, *Lord Oakburn's Daughters* 339), and openly and portentously alert the reader to family secrets, spectres from the past, and the horrors that lurk beneath domestic calm and apparent rural tranquillity. Here is a well-known, tongue-in-cheek, example from *Lady Audley's Secret*.

> We hear every day of murders committed in the country. Brutal and treacherous murders; slow, protracted agonies from poisons administered by some *kindred* hand; sudden and violent deaths by cruel blows, inflicted with a stake cut from some spreading oak, whose very shadow promised – peace. In the county of which I write, I have been shown a meadow in which, on a quiet summer Sunday evening, a young farmer murdered the girl who had loved and trusted him; and yet even now...the aspect of the spot is – peace. (*LAS* 54, emphasis added)

In the women's sensation novel (as in Collins's) the emphasis is very much on domestic violence and domestic crime: poisoning by a 'kindred' hand, crimes of passion, and intra-familial rivalries which lead to conspiracies connected to wills and the ownership of property. The women sensationalists have their fair share of male criminals – fraudsters, kidnappers, blackmailers, and even murderers – yet their most remarkable and remarked-upon criminals and wrong-doers are women: Braddon's Lady Audley, the murderous bigamist; the tempestuous Aurora Floyd, a bigamist with a tendency to horsewhip her servants; Olivia Arundel (in *John Marchmont's Legacy*), who engages in a conspiracy to kidnap the wife of the man she loves; Charlotte Carleton, the violent and possibly murderous heroine of Wood's *St Martin's Eve*, and Lady Isabel Vane, who, although not technically a criminal, is in effect guilty of crimes against womanhood and the family.

However, perhaps the most striking thing about the women writers' sensation heroine is not her criminality, but rather her deviance and transgressiveness. The sensation heroine's failure to conform to prevailing social codes is even more significant, and potentially more subversive, than her breaking of laws. Similarly, the most striking thing about the manner in which she is represented is the way in which that representation interrogates or complicates dominant ideas and images of 'Woman'. The central female characters of the women's sensation novel are of two main types: active, assertive women, who convey a sense of the threat of insurgent femininity trying to break out of the doll's house of domesticity, and passive, dependent women, who are imprisoned by it, unable to articulate their sense of confinement, and driven to desperate measures.

Many of the female sensationalists unsettle conventional images of woman by investing sympathy in, and attaching unexpected moral valuations to, particular character stereotypes. Thus, the woman who looks and ostensibly acts like the angel in the house turns out to be a demon in the house; moreover her crimes are usually committed in order to obtain socially sanctioned goals such as a good marriage. The fallen woman, who in terms of the dominant code of representation must be portrayed as a prostitute, and thus as completely beyond the moral pale, is on occasions represented more sympathetically and as more pure than the socially accepted woman who stays carefully (and, sometimes, cynically) within the bounds of convention. The heroine who conforms most closely to the feminine ideal is not idealized; she is portrayed as a victim, and the childlike innocence and clinging dependence which constitute the domestic feminine ideal are exposed as the sources of her victimhood. The women sensationalists thus engage in a complex process of negotiating, and, in the end, of revising and rewriting, that feminine tradition of submission and renunciation which was a powerful fact of both literature and life.

Nowhere is this negotiation of conventional images of femininity more apparent than in the women sensationalists' representation of motherhood. Maternity is in many ways the key to the representation of femininity in virtually all forms of

Victorian discourse. The ideological constructs of femininity, womanhood and womanliness were all defined through the maternal function of biological females. The dominant characteristics of this version of femininity, from hysteria to spiritual refinement, from a potentially engulfing sexuality to self-sacrificing affectivity, were 'deemed equally the products of the uterine economy'.[22] The various versions of motherhood that pervade the women's sensation novel include: absent (dead) mothers, neglectful mothers, abandoning mothers, over-invested mothers who neglect their husbands, mothers who spoil their children with an excess of indulgent love (often with disastrous consequences, when that child is a son), mothers who challenge Victorian conceptions of the feminine ideal by being murderers.

As well as the mother, the motherless girl is an important figure in the women's sensation novel, as Margaret Oliphant noted: 'Ill-brought-up motherless girls, left to grow anyhow, out of all feminine guardianship, have become the ideal of the novelist'.[23] The lack of a mother renders the sensation heroine both more assertive and independent and/or more vulnerable than the woman who has been conventionally socialized under the surveillance and guidance of a mother. Aurora Floyd's wildness, for example, is attributed to the lack of that careful mothering required to 'train and prune' the 'exuberant branches' which develop in women in their natural state, and which must be 'trimmed and clipped and fastened primly to the stone wall of society with cruel nails' (*AF* 50). As Braddon's horticultural metaphor suggests, the women sensationalists are much preoccupied with the relationship between woman in her 'natural' state and the socialized forms of femininity.

MARY ELIZABETH BRADDON

Mary Elizabeth Braddon was widely acknowledged as the uncrowned queen of the sensation novel, who, as a writer in the *North British Review* put it in 1865, was possessed of a power to bewitch the 'unthinking crowd'.[24] Braddon was well prepared for this role by her earlier career as an actress and her continuing career as a jobbing writer of thrilling stories and serials for the penny dreadfuls. She took to the stage probably at the age of seventeen[25] to help support her mother whose husband deserted her when Braddon was a young child. By 1860 she was established in London, furiously penning pulp for cheap working-class magazines, a practice she kept up even after her success as a sensationalist. Braddon wrote constantly in order to earn enough money to support herself, her partner (the publisher John Maxwell), their five illegitimate children, and the children of his legal marriage (Maxwell's wife, in an uncanny echo of the sensation plot, was an inmate of a Dublin lunatic asylum).

Clearly Braddon's knowledge of the repertoire of the stage melodrama provided her with fictional subjects and situations. Moreover, some of the effects of her practical experience of staging can be seen in the style and structure of her sensation novels, not least in her frequent use of dramatic tableaux. Although she was always carefully chaperoned by her mother, the unconventional life of an actress also exposed her to an experience which was rather wider and freer than that usually available to the middle-class girl who grew up in the drawing-room under the strict surveillance of the maternal eye. As Henry James pointed out in his appreciative early review of Braddon's novels, 'she knows much that ladies are not accustomed to know, but that they are apparently very glad to learn'.[26] Similarly, Braddon's experience of writing for lower-class magazines gave her a facility for recycling other people's plots and developing endless variations on the same themes. As she explained to Bulwer Lytton, who had developed his own brand of sensationalism in the 1830s, 'the amount of crime, treachery, murder, slow poisoning, and general infamy required by the halfpenny reader is something terrible'.[27]

Braddon, like Ellen Wood, 'Ouida', Rhoda Broughton and other women writers who were reviewed as sensation novelists in the 1860s , enjoyed a long career as a writer; the last of around ninety novels was published posthumously in 1916. Despite her earnest wish to be regarded as a serious artist, and notwith-standing her adoption of a wide range of genres and styles (including melodrama, naturalism, romance, domestic realism, social satire, the novel of manners and the historical novel), Braddon was always something of a sensationalist, repeatedly reverting to the character types, scenes, plots and incidents of the sensation novel throughout her career. She was also to some degree always a satirist, whose witty satirization or mockery of social and literary modes contributed a great deal to her originality and force as a sensationalist. Braddon rarely simply repeated the formulas of the sensation novel; she was engaged in a constant process of negotiation and revision of its conventions. She parodied and satirized sensationalism, and she was a commentator on its power and its foibles, as can be seen in her letters to Bulwer Lytton, in the comments she provided for her mouthpiece Sigismund Smith, a sensation novelist who first appears in *The Doctor's Wife* and who reappears as Sigismund Smyth in *The Lady's Mile* (1866), and in the pages of *Belgravia: A London Magazine* which began publication, under her editorship, in 1866.

Like most sensation novels, Braddon's sensation narratives have their origins in female imperfection. As the narrator remarks of Aurora Floyd:

> [I]f she had been faultless she could not have been the heroine of this story; for has not some wise old man of old remarked, that the perfect women are those who leave no histories behind them. (*AF* 393)

Braddon's heroines are, for one reason or another, not what they seem. Most of her sensation narratives are structured around women with something to hide, some secret in the past which makes their present life a sham or masquerade. In several cases that secret is a family secret connected with the heroine's father, who is, at best, weak, vain, neglectful of his family responsibilities and exploitative of his daughter. At worst, he is a criminal whose guilt both compromises the heroine's social respectability and produces in her a sense of guilt by association. In such cases – for example, in *Eleanor's Victory, Run To Earth, Henry Dunbar* and *The Doctor's Wife* – the heroine tends to conceal her father's true nature from herself and/or to conceal his existence from the world. The plots of these novels are constructed around the complexities and contradictions of women's conflicting familial roles as daughters, wives and mothers.

In some of Braddon's most powerful novels, the secrets which drive the narrative are those of the heroine's own criminal past, or of her dark and demonic depths. Examples include Braddon's two most famous successes, *Lady Audley's Secret* and *Aurora Floyd*, and also *John Marchmont's Legacy*, which contains, in Olivia Arundel, one of the most remarkable representations of a daughter of the vicarage to be found in Victorian fiction. *Lady Audley's Secret*, Braddon's mischievous reworking of *The Woman in White*, was greeted as 'one of the most noxious books of modern times'[28] because of its portrayal of the sweetly smiling, golden-haired Lucy Graham (formerly Helen Maldon, later Helen Talboys and finally Lady Audley), who was 'at once the heroine and the monstrosity of the novel',[29] a Lady Macbeth in the shape of the feminine ideal; 'the lovely woman with the fishy extremities' as the reviewer in *The Times* put it.[30]

> Wherever she went she seemed to take joy and brightness with her. In the cottages of the poor her fair face shone like a sunbeam . . . [she] was blessed with that magic power of fascination by which a woman can charm with a word or intoxicate with a smile. Every one loved, admired, and praised her. (*LAS* 5–6)

Lucy Graham is certainly not what she seems, but she plays the part of the submissive, complaisant, feminine ideal so well that she captivates a foolish old baronet, and almost everyone in sight. Female 'fascination' and the power of the myth of the feminine ideal sustain Lucy's masquerade for much of the novel. The reader too is fascinated, but also disturbed. The representation of Lady Audley is a bold assault on the reader's preconceptions about women in both literature and life. It satirizes the feminine ideal by exaggerating it, while also, at the same time, dramatizing numerous anxieties about that cultural ideal and about the 'natural' female forces which it is designed to keep in check. *Lady Audley's Secret* pleases, thrills, shocks and undermines its readers with the fact that this personification of simpering, charitable, childlike, genteel femininity is, in fact, a cold, calculating, resourceful woman, who abandons her child and is capable of murder, all in the interests of self-help and self-preservation. The irony is that all of Lucy's actions are directed towards those goals which were recommended to all middle-class girls: achieving and maintaining a socially acceptable and financially secure marriage, and keeping up appearances.

Braddon represents Lucy as an actress and a chameleon, and thus plays on the reader's fears and fantasies about women's duplicity. Before the action of the novel begins, Lucy, as Helen Maldon, the daughter of a disreputable half-pay naval officer, has made what she thinks is a socially advantageous marriage, only to discover that her outraged father-in-law has disinherited her husband, who promptly leaves to seek his fortunes in Australia – a continent of immense usefulness to Victorian novelists in need of a convenient black hole in which to make characters disappear. Lucy (now Helen Talboys) does not go into a decline to await rescue by some shining knight, nor does she fall onto the streets, as she might if she really were the vulnerable, childlike woman she appears. Instead, she carefully stages her own death, complete with *Times* obituary notice, reinvents herself as Lucy Graham, writes herself some references and obtains a post as a governess, leaving her infant son with her father.

Is she mad, or is she just bad? The novel blurs the issue. Viewed from one end of the telescope of the Victorian ideology of femininity, Helen/Lucy's histrionics are but another version of that hysteria to which all women are prone – the product of puerperal fever perhaps, or the insanity which she claims she has inherited from her mother. Viewed from the other end of the telescope, Helen/Lucy's role-playing is a particular form of Victorian self-help and self-fashioning:

> I had learnt that which in some indefinite manner or other *every schoolgirl learns sooner or later* – I learned that my ultimate fate in life depended upon my marriage, and I concluded that if I was indeed prettier than my schoolfellows, I ought to marry better than any of them. (*LAS* 350, emphasis added)

A girl has to do what a girl has to do, when marriage is the most secure career choice open to the genteel woman. What is shocking is that Lucy not only does it, she acknowledges it.

If the feminine ideal is an illusion, even a fraud, what then is conventional marriage, which is produced by and which reproduces that ideal? This novel provides some discomforting answers in its representation of a marriage built on a tissue of lies, impersonation, fraud and murder. As in Collins's sensation novels, the detection of this dreadful secret is mainly the work of a man who polices the family; in this case the family policeman is Robert Audley, Sir Michael's nephew. Robert is a familiar type in the sensation novel; a type produced by the genre's preoccupation with the construction of gendered identities, and by its complex juxtapositioning of aristocratic and bourgeois values. Robert, like Collins's Walter Hartright and Franklin Blake, begins the novel as a liminal figure who lacks a masculine identity and vocation. He is supposedly reading for the Bar, but is actually spending his time in a state of feminized, aristocratic indolence, reading French novels – always a dangerous sign in Victorian fiction. As in Collins's novels the route to masculinity is the discovery of the secrets of the family, and the simultaneous discovery of a vocation and a commitment to the work ethic. For Robert the family becomes his work. In his efforts to solve the mysteries of his friend George Talboys's disappearance and his 'dead' wife, and to penetrate the secrets of Lady Audley, Robert develops those forensic legal skills, such as assembling documents and marshalling a logical case, that he had found tedious before he discovered a motive for his existence. The motive force for Robert's journey to a properly socialized bourgeois masculinity is a woman, or rather, two women: the 'fascinating' and bewitching Lady Audley, who merely impersonates the feminine ideal, and George's sister, Clara Talboys, who actually is the feminine ideal. Robert's discovery of Clara begins the process by which he reconstructs his feminized identity, represses his attraction to Lady Audley's dangerous femininity, and expels it from the family.

In one of Braddon's most interesting reworkings of the plot of *The Woman in White*, she has her hero re-enact the role that Collins gave to his villain. In Collins's novel the hero rescues victimized women from the lunatic asylums to which they have been consigned by a villain who wants to gain control of their wealth or prevent them from telling his secrets. In Braddon's novel, on the other hand, the hero plots to have a woman incarcerated in a lunatic asylum, to prevent the revelation of her own secrets. Having constructed his own route to masculinity and commitment to the family by exposing his aunt's secrets, Robert suppresses them. The versions of femininity on which his newly discovered masculinity is constructed can contain the madwoman, but not the murderess. Containing disruptive femininity is what the conclusion of the Lucy Audley plot is all about. Robert's discussions with doctors expose the way in which madness was used by the Victorian medical profession as a convenient way of labelling and managing disruptive femininity. As the medical expert called in by Robert puts it: 'The lady is not mad...She has the cunning of madness, with the prudence of intelligence. I will tell you what she is...She is dangerous!' (*LAS* 379).

Braddon also uses madness as a way of figuring dangerous femininity in her portrayal of Olivia Arundel in *John Marchmont's Legacy*. Whereas Lucy Audley's mask of the passionless woman of the feminine ideal conceals cold, prudential calculation, Olivia's conventional (even conventual) appearance and her role as the dutiful daughter of the vicarage mask a darkly passionate nature. Lady Audley's story ends with her containment in a lunatic asylum, modelled on the bourgeois household in order that the middle-class family and the feminine ideal on which it is constructed may be defended from the threat she presents. Olivia, on the other hand, is represented as the prisoner of that ideal and that model of the family. If *Lady Audley's Secret* raises the question of whether madness is simply a label that is attached to deviant femininity, *John Marchmont's Legacy* raises the even more interesting question of whether madness is a *symptom* of bourgeois femininity.

Olivia Arundel cherishes a passionate and secret love for her cousin Edward, but she has an even better kept secret – 'the bitter discontent grown fierce and mad' (as Carlyle wrote of the working classes in his essay 'Chartism', published in 1839) of her 'fearfully monotonous, narrow and uneventful life' (*JML* 68) as the daughter of the aptly named Swampington Rectory in the gloomy Lincolnshire countryside. Olivia is a fascinating portrait of female repression, a 'woman who ought to have been a great man', but who instead must live her life within a 'narrow boundary':

> from infancy to womanhood...performing and repeating the same duties from day to day, with no other progress to mark the lapse of her existence than the slow alternation of the seasons, and the dark hollow circles which had lately deepened beneath her grey eyes...These outward tokens, beyond her control, alone betrayed this woman's secret. She was weary of her life. She sickened under [its] dull burden...The slow round of duty was loathsome to her. The horrible, narrow, unchanging existence, shut in by cruel walls

which bounded her in on every side and kept her prisoner to herself, was odious to her. The powerful intellect revolted against the fetters that bound and galled it. The proud heart beat with murderous violence against the bonds that kept it captive. (*JML* 68)

This is powerful stuff by any standards, and likely to produce a complex response of recognition and rebuttal in the nineteenth-century woman reader. Of course, in the end readers are meant to reject Olivia, who is driven to intrigue and crime by her thwarted nature and her frustrated love for her cousin Edward. Before we do, however, we have more than a pang of sympathy for this wasted life, confined by the iron chains of convention.

The lengthy passage quoted above is evidence of Braddon's self-professed admiration for the 'Balzac morbid anatomy school', as she put it in a letter to Edmund Yates.[31] It is also typical of the melodramatic excess of her own sensation style. Braddon habitually uses this style in the set-piece scenes and dramatic tableaux which display her main female characters to the reader's gaze as a form of spectacle. The reader is repeatedly invited to look at the central female character, or to look at the narrator or the other characters looking at her. The most obvious example of this specularity is Braddon's use of the pre-Raphaelite portrait of Lady Audley in the eighth chapter of *Lady Audley's Secret*. The reader views this portrait over the shoulder of George Talboys, who (with Robert Audley) has secretly gained access to Lucy's boudoir where it is located. The reader does not view the portrait through the eyes of George – who merely stares at the portrait for fifteen minutes in blank silence. Rather the portrait is displayed to the reader and 'read' by the narrator, who both satirizes pre-Raphaelitism –'No one but a pre-Raphaelite would have painted, hair by hair, those feathery masses of ringlets with every glimmer of gold, and every shadow of pale brown' – and simultaneously appropriates and redeploys the pre-Raphaelite gaze. George's blank stare (so we discover later) has acquainted him with the real identity of Lady Audley (as Helen Talboys), while the knowing narrator offers the sensuous and sensual portrait as revealing or unmasking her identity as a 'beautiful fiend':

> It was so like and yet so unlike; it was as if you had burned strange-coloured fires before my lady's face, and by their influence brought out new lines and new expressions never seen in it before....

> Her crimson dress…hung about her in folds that looked like
> flames, her fair head peeping out of the lurid mass of colour, as if out
> of a raging furnace…the ripe scarlet of the pouting lips…all
> combined to render the first effect of the painting by no means an
> agreeable one.

Braddon's representation of this portrait also demonstrates, as
Anne Cvetkovich has argued, how sensational representation
works more generally, deriving its power from 'rendering
concrete or visible what would otherwise be hidden':

> If Lady Audley looked as evil as she supposedly is, she would be less
> sensational…The sensation of repulsion produced by Lady Audley's
> criminality is indistinguishable from the fascination produced by her
> beauty; sensationalism consists in the indistinguishability of the two
> feelings.[32]

Many contemporary reviewers complained about the sen-
suality and sexual depravity of Braddon's heroines. This is an
interesting displacement since, on the whole, Braddon's women
seem remarkably uninterested in sex, especially when they are
compared, for example, with Rhoda Broughton's creations, who
exist in a permanent state of throbbing palpitation, before going
into a decline, worn out with (for the most part) unconsummated passion. For example, the passions of Lady Audley are
most in evidence when defending the social position and
material trappings which accompany marriage to a baronet.

> The common temptations that assail and shipwreck some women
> had no terror for me…The mad folly that the world calls love had
> never any part in my madness, and here at least extremes met and
> the vice of heartlessness became the virtue of constancy. (*LAS* 354)

In fact, on the whole, Braddon's women tend to be presented not
as desiring, sexual subjects, but as sexual objects. This is partly an
effect of the regime of looking, and of the dominant codes for
representing the female body in nineteenth-century writing and
painting.[33] Braddon's novels repeatedly represent their female
characters through their physical appearance, especially their hair
– a fetishism much commented upon and derided by Victorian
reviewers. Olivia Arundel's hair is both sign and symptom of her
failure to conform to the feminine ideal:

> Those masses of hair had not that purple lustre, nor yet that
> wandering glimmer of red gold, which gives peculiar beauty to some

raven tresses. Olivia's hair was long and luxuriant; but it was of that dead, inky blackness, which is all shadow. It was dark, fathomless, inscrutable, like herself.[34] (JML 71)

The impetuous, inadvertent-bigamist heroine of *Aurora Floyd* is the object of a similar treatment. In Aurora's case the mode of representation is doubly voyeuristic, since the reader is usually invited to watch someone watching Aurora. The heroine is first seen through the eyes of Talbot Bulstrode, her first suitor, who rejects her when he hears rumours of her youthful escapades in Paris. To Bulstrode, the embodiment of muscular manliness – complete with aristocratic pedigree and a closed mind on the woman question – Aurora appears as 'A divinity! imperiously beautiful in white and scarlet, painfully dazzling to look upon, intoxicatingly brilliant to behold' (AF 33). The gap between masculine fantasies of divine womanhood and the untidy realities of actual women is brought home sharply by the words uttered by this apparition: 'Do you know if Thunderbolt won the Leger?'

This voyeuristic form of representation is used, in part, to explore different ways of perceiving femininity. The differing perceptions of Bulstrode and John Mellish are interestingly juxtaposed, particularly their perceptions of the striking, racy, 'Girl of the Period' Aurora and her blonde cousin Lucy, the rather insipid personification of the feminine ideal. The voyeuristic method is also used as a means of controlling the reader's response both to Aurora, and to the version of femininity she represents. Thus at the crux of the narrative, when the unravelling of Aurora's 'miserable secrets' has brought her to 'the threshold of darker miseries', the reader is invited to join John Mellish in watching the unwitting heroine as she sleeps.

> Aurora was lying on the sofa, wrapped in a loose white dressing-gown, her masses of ebon hair uncoiled and falling about her shoulders in serpentine tresses that looked like shining blue-black snakes released from poor Medusa's head to make their escape amid the folds of her garment. (AF 271)

This pre-Raphaelite word-painting pictures Aurora as an object of erotic desire and, at the same time, a non-threatening, self-contained, almost auto-erotic creature (the snakes, for example, are burying themselves in her clothes, not directed outwards to the spectator). Readers, male and female alike, are thus offered a pleasurable image of female erotic power, but one whose potential danger is defused and contained by framing, just as Aurora herself is eventually framed by the family and contained by motherhood.

Aurora is ultimately rescued for domestic womanhood by an ordeal of suffering and by maternity. First, Aurora's disruptive femininity is contained by the threatened loss of her home and husband, and she is brought within the boundaries of the womanly behaviour which she has hitherto despised and refused. During this process the reader is positioned as the spectator of Aurora's drama of suffering, and is the recipient of the narrator's woman-to-woman address on the heroine's predicament.

> Ah, careless wives! who think it a small thing, perhaps, that your husbands are honest and generous, constant and true, and who are apt to grumble because your neighbours have started a carriage ... stop and think of this wretched girl, who in this hour of desolation recalled a thousand little wrongs she had done to her husband, and would have laid herself under his feet to be walked over by him could she have thus atoned for her petty tyrannies ... Think of her in her loneliness, with her heart yearning to go back to the man she loved. (*AF* 345)

This passage works to reinforce conventional womanly virtues by directly addressing both the reader's possible marital discontents and her guilt at her own womanly failings. By allowing the female reader to identify with a socially and sexually transgressive woman, it also allows her to experience vicariously the frisson of having lost the benefits of the love of an honest and good man – benefits which, by implication, are undervalued by the conventional bourgeois wife. Although this novel speaks with several voices on the marriage question – for example, the conventionally ideal marriage of Talbot Bulstrode and the fair Lucy comes in for some particularly good understated satire – the effect of this passage is to 'talk up' the value of ordinary marriage.

The second step in Aurora's redemption for womanliness is her embracing of the maternal role. *Aurora Floyd* thus offers a challenging and exciting, even seductive image of the 'Girl of the Period' before putting her back in place – albeit with a touch of parody – as the repentant wife and doting mother: 'a little changed, a shade less defiantly bright, but unspeakably beautiful and tender, bending over the cradle of her first-born' (*AF* 459). Aurora (and the woman reader) is, in this novel, if not in life, allowed to have it all, although not all at once: a racy, adventurous youth followed by marriage to an adoring man, and doting motherhood.

Helen/Lucy, Aurora and Olivia are all motherless daughters who in various ways disown or rebel against their fathers and each of them is a woman-with-a-secret, whose secret is connected to her own misdeeds and hidden desires. The secrecy, concealment and disguise of the motherless heroines of *Eleanor's Victory* and *Henry Dunbar*, on the other hand, derive from their loyalty to their selfish, wayward or downright criminal fathers. In *Henry Dunbar*, for example, the secrecy and disguise of the heroine, Margaret Wentworth, results from her collusion in concealing her father's murder and impersonation of his former employer. This misplaced filial loyalty is responsible for the many narrative complications which temporarily impede Margaret's progress from daughter to wife. In *Eleanor's Victory*, on the other hand, the heroine engages in concealment in order to carry out the covert detection that will enable her to avenge the death of her father, who is presented to the reader as a manipulative wastrel. Both her desire for revenge and the process by which she seeks to achieve it are condemned by Eleanor's surrogate brother Richard Thornton as likely 'to waste your life, blight your girlhood, unsex your mind, and transform you from a candid and confiding woman into an amateur detective'.[35] Like Magdalen Vanstone, the heroine of Collins's *No Name* (which began its serial run in *All The Year Round* exactly a year before the first instalment of *Eleanor's Victory* in *Once A Week*), Eleanor marries a man she does not love, Gilbert Monckton, in order to be able to observe more closely the painter Launcelot Darrell, who has also proposed marriage to her, and whom she suspects of causing her father's death. Like *No Name*, Braddon's narrative propels its heroine into the world of the theatre and into situations in which she must take the initiative and live by her wits, before reaching a resolution in which, in common with many other sensation heroines, she acknowledges the value of the love of a good man and accepts a 'feminine' social and familial role. Like other sensation novels, including *Aurora Floyd*, several of the plot complications of *Eleanor's Victory* involve marital misunderstandings, and a husband's erroneous suspicions of his wife's adultery. Like Aurora, Eleanor only learns to love her husband after she has married him and after the marriage has been threatened. The narrative concludes by reuniting Eleanor with Monckton, who had left her after misreading her obsession with Darrell as an adulterous love, and by bringing Eleanor to an acceptance of a 'feminine' role after a period of impersonating the 'masculine' one of detective. Having discovered that Darrell was indeed guilty both of cheating her father at cards and forging a will, but that he was not guilty of his murder, Eleanor not only renounces her scheme of vengeance against him but she also responds positively to an appeal from his mother to treat him as she would wish her own (putative) children to be treated in similar circumstances. The novel ends with a rhetorical flourish from the narrator:

> after all, Eleanor's Victory was a proper womanly conquest, and not a stern, classical vengeance. The tender woman's heart triumphed over the girl's rash vow; and poor George Vane's enemy was left to the only Judge whose judgments are always righteous.[36]

Several contemporary reviewers objected to what they saw as a weak ending which appeared to have been tacked on to avoid offending 'the moral sense of a Christian public'.[37] W. Fraser Rae, on the other hand, was offended by Braddon's handling of the renunciation of vengeance on the grounds that it left a story whose moral seemed to be 'that to cheat a old man at cards and to forge a will are no impediments to attaining distinction in the world, and, indeed, are rather venial offences'.[38] The 'moral' of the ending, and of the narrator's glossing of it are rather more complex than Rae concedes. Eleanor's victory is not simply that she has ceded to God what is properly his – 'Vengeance is mine; I will repay, saith the Lord' [Romans 12:19] – nor that she has meted out womanly charity and forgiveness to Darrell, but also that she has conquered herself and her own unwomanly impulses to lead an active and independent life.

Having shot to success, fame, and even notoriety as a sensation author in the first few years of the 1860s, Braddon felt herself to be unfairly singled out for attack by 'that set of critics' who 'pelted me with the word "sensational"' as she put it in a letter to Edward Bulwer Lytton.[39] She sought to answer these critics by means of a vigorous campaign both in her novels and in the pages of the magazine *Belgravia*, which she edited from 1866 until 1876. Her first concerted engagement with her critics, and with the anti-sensationalists more generally, was in *The Doctor's Wife* (1864), both in her witty and sympathetic portrayal of Sigismund Smith the writer of popular serials and 'combination novels', and in her attempt to by-pass the sensation genre by adapting for an English setting and a middlebrow audience the plot of Flaubert's story of adultery in the provinces, *Madame Bovary* (1857). Unlike Braddon's earlier successes and Sigismund's frantically produced offerings for his 'penny public', *The Doctor's Wife* did not seek to supply (as Smith would have it) 'plot and plenty of it; surprises and plenty of 'em; mystery as thick as a November fog' (*DW* 45). There are no lost wills, kidnappings, elopements or bigamy in this novel. Nor does the story of Isabel Gilbert's disappointment in her marriage to a worthy but dull country doctor, and her subsequent love for the aristocratic poet, Roland Landsell, end in adultery; indeed, however implausibly, the heroine does not appear to see this outcome as a possibility. Certainly the use of the heroine's criminal father as the nemesis of her would-be seducer is a sensation device, and was roundly condemned as such by critics. However, for the most part, this is a relatively plotless and incident-free story of provincial life whose main preoccupation is an exploration of the role of reading in the formation and subsequent moral and sentimental education of its heroine. Braddon's narrator reverses the usual argument that it was novels, and particularly sensation novels, which gave women readers an inappropriate knowledge of sexual matters and led them into disreputable behaviour – and in the process directs a sly dig at Braddon's critics – when she attributes Isabel's naivety to the fact that she is more familiar with novels than with newspapers:

> A woman of the world would have very quickly perceived that Mr. Lansdell's discourse must have relation to more serious projects than future meetings under Lord Thurston's oak, with interchange of divers volumes of light literature. But Isabel Gilbert was not a

woman of the world. She had read novels while other people perused the Sunday papers; and of the world out of a three-volume romance she had no more idea than a baby. She believed in a phantasmal universe, created out of the pages of poets and romancers; she knew that there were good people and bad people...but beyond this she had very little notion of mankind. (*DW* 252–3)

Isabel's chosen reading is far from disreputable. Her favourite novels are those of Bulwer Lytton, Dickens, and Thackeray and she also reads poetry, specifically the high culture, if sensational, poems of Byron (*Corsair* and *Giaour*) and Shelley (*Revolt of Islam*), and also *An Alien's Dreams*, by a nameless poet who turns out to be Roland Lansdell. Whatever her chosen form or genre, Isabel begins the novel as a 'bad reader' who loses herself in books – a reading practice of which critics accused the readers of sensation fiction. Her story is, in large part, the story of how she becomes a more engaged and productive reader.

Far from silencing her critics *The Doctor's Wife* provoked W. Fraser Rae to declare that it proved that 'she is a slave, as it were, to the style she created. "Sensation" is her Frankenstein'.[40] Braddon continued to seek to answer her critics whilst also satisfying 'my own public which demands strong meat'[41] in her novels for *Belgravia*. For example, the linked novels *Birds of Prey* (1867) and *Charlotte's Inheritance* (1868) both combined sensation with social satire. Both novels used the sensation staples of murder and slow poisoning, deception, concealment, theft, and hidden identity in an extremely complicated plot which depends on both the ability of 'gentlemanly vulture[s]' to mask their villainy with an appearance of 'eminent respectability' and the inability of the passive, overly trustful women who are their victims to read against the grain of respectable appearances. In these novels the chief demon in the house is not a thwarted or ambitious woman but a medical man, Philip Sheldon, 'a thorough-paced scoundrel in a quiet gentlemanly way'.[42] Sheldon's first victim is his friend Tom Halliday, whose wife and fortune he desires. His second intended victim is Tom's daughter, Charlotte, now Sheldon's step-daughter and the heir to a substantial inheritance. Sheldon practises a form of slow poisoning in the guise of treating his victims for nervous illness: Charlotte's nerves, she laments, 'are the beginning and end of mischief... if I could get the better of my nerves, I should be as well as ever'.[43]

As well as using *Belgravia* as a vehicle for sensational novels about the dangers of respectable appearances and not getting the better of one's nerves, Braddon also used her position as editor of this magazine to conduct a defence of sensation fiction and other 'light literature' and to attack those high-brow critics and periodicals that set themselves up as cultural police. As Jennifer Phegley and Solveig Robinson have so clearly shown,[44] Braddon used both the fiction and essay content of *Belgravia* to educate her readers about the use and value of 'light literature' and the critical practices and standards that were appropriate to it. In particular two articles she commissioned from George Augustus Sala were deployed to launch a counterattack on Margaret Oliphant's anonymous hostile review of novels by Braddon, Broughton and other sensation novelists in *Blackwoods* in September 1867, to attack the cant of modern criticism in general, and to mount a defence of the sensation novel. In 'The Cant of Modern Criticism' and 'On the Sensational in Literature and Art' Sala repositioned the sensation novel from the margins to the centre of culture by constructing a long sensation tradition which included both high and low culture and which, in the nineteenth century, included such figures as Dickens, Millais, Ruskin and Darwin, as well as Braddon. All great art was sensational, he argued, 'everything is "sensational" that is vivid, and nervous, and forcible, and graphic, and true'.[45] Sala positioned sensation fiction at the cutting edge of culture, citing Braddon, George Eliot (in *Adam Bede*) and Charlotte Brontë (in *Jane Eyre*) as sensation authors, who were producing or had produced 'the modern, the contemporary novel of life and character and adventure – the outspoken, realistic, moving, breathing fiction which mirrors the passions of the age for which it is written'.[46] Writing as 'Babington White' Braddon herself made the link between the sensation novel and high culture in satirical form in 'The Mudies Classics' in *Belgravia*. Here she offered to provide tales modelled on 'the highest exemplars of art', in deference to those authorities whose 'critical contempt for all stories of a sensational character has of late become a fact so notorious that the conductor of this magazine would be wanting in deference to those great

Teachers who preside over the Literary Journals of this country, if she failed to recognize the necessity of an immediate reform in the class of fiction provided'.[47] Of course the Greek dramas which are offered for the reform of sensation fiction are full of matricide, bigamy, adultery and murder, the very things for which sensation fiction was condemned.

In 1873 Maxwell sold the serial rights of Braddon's latest novel *Taken At The Flood* to the Lancashire newspaper owner W.F. Tillotson, who syndicated its weekly publication in a dozen local newspapers, prior to publication in volume form. Braddon was the first well-known British novelist to sign up for this model of publication which was to dominate the serial market for the next twenty years. Braddon remained Tillotson's leading author until the end of the 1880s, when she moved to Leng's – another syndication agency. The dozen or so novels that she sold to Tillotson continued to deploy the sensation formula which had contributed to her fame and infamy in the 1860s, the main difference being as Law and Maunder note that 'her transgressive heroines... tend to be more introspective than in the days of Lady Audley and Aurora Floyd'.[48] Many of these novels were both marketed and reviewed as sensation novels.

A Strange World (1875), whose actress heroine is partly based on Braddon's stage experience, is a sensation novel set in the 1860s. It is a tale of love, murder, blackmail and detection, which also includes a mad mother and a suicide. In this case the sensation novel's preoccupations with a woman with a secret and an inheritance plot come together when the secret of the heroine's birth is uncovered to reveal that she is the rightful heir of the estate whose possession had been a motive for murder. In *Joshua Haggard's Daughter* (1876) a sensational plot involving a murder prompted by suspicion of adultery is balanced by a careful, realistic characterization of the main protagonists – Joshua Haggard, his much younger second wife, his daughter and her husband. Increasingly in the 1880s and 1890s Braddon combined sensation with the new vogue for crime and detection. *Wyllard's Weird*, syndicated in 1884 and published in volume form in 1885 is a good example of this. The novel opens with the mysterious death of a young girl who falls from a train, a mystery which deepens when the dead girl is linked to a double murder committed some ten years earlier. The mystery is unravelled in a range of rural and urban settings: a Cornish village, the backstreets of Paris, aristocratic estates, the haunts of journalists and the homes of Bohemian artists. Like Braddon's earlier sensation novels it questions the sanctity of marriage and exposes the vices concealed by genteel surfaces. The syndicated serial version of this novel was advertised as 'A NEW AND EXCITING SENSATION NOVEL BY MISS BRADDON',[49] and when it appeared in volume form the *Athenaeum* reviewed it as an example of the recent revival of sensation fiction:

> It is obvious that current fiction is suffering from a revival. The tales of mystery and murder which went out of fashion as art came in are beginning to captivate once more... It was not to be expected that the author of 'Lady Audley's Secret' should look on while others won success in the field where she had triumphed twenty years ago.[50]

Like and Unlike (1887), updates a melodramatic-sensational story of rivalry in love, elopement, murder and its concealment, and the redemption of the murderer by a good woman by making the erring wife one of the new style of fast girls, and by the use of a photograph in proving the murderer's guilt. *Thou Art The Man* (1894) involves Coralie Urquhart's careful unravelling of an extremely tangled and sensational tale of secret relationships, murder, wrongful incarceration in an asylum, madness and coercion. Coralie is not only one of Braddon's many amateur detectives, she is also one of several daughters who uncovers the secrets of her father's guilt. Another of Braddon's detective-sensation novels, *Rough Justice* (1898), deploys both an amateur and a professional detective in a plot which revolves around the sensation staples of secret relationships and illegitimate children. This late novel is unusual among Braddon's works in having a split narrative in which the third person narrative alternates with the first person narrative of the police detective Faunce.

ELLEN WOOD

> It is not pleasant to write of these things... but I know of few histories where they can be entirely avoided, if the whole truth has to be adhered to, for many and evil are the passions that assail the undisciplined human heart.[51]

'Pleasant' or not, the passions of 'the undisciplined human heart', and the processes by which women and men learn to govern them, or – more interestingly – succumb to them, provide the sensational material of Ellen Wood's otherwise sentimental novels. A bald summary of the core of the plot of *East Lynne* might make it appear to be the most outrageous of the sensation novels of the early sixties. Its heroine, Lady Isabel Vane is a beautiful and refined young woman, who, left penniless on the death of her wastrel father, marries Archibald Carlyle, a decent, hard-working, country solicitor only to desert him and her infant children to elope with an aristocratic seducer, whose illegitimate child she bears after he has deserted her. So far, so shocking. However, the wages of all this sinning turn out, after all (reassuringly), to be death. The erring heroine is made an example to would-be straying wives.

Despite her errant behaviour Isabel remains the novel's heroine. She is represented as a sinner rather than a villain or criminal, and she retains the readers' (if not most reviewers') sympathies to the end. In many ways sympathy for Isabel's sufferings and for the complexities of her predicament actually increases as her social and moral standing declines. *East Lynne*, like several of Wood's other novels of the 1860s, is, Winifred Hughes has asserted, an example of the sensation novel as 'pure soap opera, loaded down with pathos, disaster, tortures of guilt and repentance'.[52] However, like modern film or television soap opera it offers a complex range of messages, meanings and satisfactions to its audience. *East Lynne* is not the straightforwardly simple tale of pious, conventional morality that it appears to be at first sight.

It is easy to understand why some early reviewers of *East Lynne* should have seen it as an example of the sensation novel's obsession with women intent on doing as they like, and loving whom they like. *East Lynne* is, after all, the story of an adulteress. However, when this novel dwells on the sensations of its heroine, it dwells less on her sensual longings for male muscles, and more on her frustrated maternal feelings. One of the main narrative functions of Isabel's adultery is to produce the circumstances which give rise to that 'prolonged and luxurious orgy of self-torture'[53] which constitutes the most powerful part of the novel. *East Lynne* is, importantly, the story of a wife and mother, and of a mother's sufferings. This is a powerfully appealing theme, particularly to women readers, and especially at a time when motherhood and womanhood and the links between the two, were being hotly contested. One of the novel's central contrasts is that between the two wives of Archibald Carlyle: the aristocratic Isabel Vane, who gives way to feeling, suffers and dies, and the bourgeois Barbara Hare, a woman who learns to control her powerful feelings, not least those of jealousy, and survives.

A particularly significant point of contrast between Isabel and Barbara is their differing responses to motherhood. Barbara, the second Mrs Carlyle is a rational, modern mother. Her conduct as a wife and mother, and her views on these roles seem to come straight out of the conduct books and advice manuals for women which proliferated in the nineteenth century. Thus, in a moment of exquisitely poignant irony, the second Mrs Carlyle addresses the first Mrs Carlyle (in her disguise as governess to her own children) on the subject of family management:

> I hold an opinion...that too many mothers pursue a mistaken system in the management of their family. There are some, we know, who, lost in the pleasures of the world, in frivolity, wholly neglect them...nothing can be more thoughtless...but there are others who err on the opposite side. They are never happy but when with their children. They wash them, dress them, feed them...[such a mother] loses her authority...The discipline of that house soon becomes broken. The children run wild; the husband is sick of it, and seeks peace and solace elsewhere...I shall never give up to another...the training of my children...This is a mother's task. (EL 407)

Mrs Sarah Ellis, whose books on the conduct of the wives, daughters and mothers of England were extremely influential in the mid-nineteenth century, put the matter more succinctly:

> wherever a mother thus doats upon her children, she is guilty of an act of unfaithfulness to her husband, at the same time that she places herself in a perilous position, from whence the first shock of disease, or the first symptom of ingratitude, may cast her down into utter wretchedness.[54]

Isabel is an example of the doting mother, whose first act of unfaithfulness to her husband (with her children) is quickly followed by her adultery with Levison. However, the contrast between the two Mrs Carlyles is not a simple one. Even as Barbara is mouthing the conduct book moralisms which are the source of her survival – moralisms with which many contemporary readers would have been educated to agree – the novel's readers are also being positioned so as to identify and sympathize with the sufferings of Isabel, the over-invested or doting mother. Morally the reader is asked to approve of Barbara's bourgeois prudence, which 'proves' itself more serviceable by winning the day. Emotionally, however, the readers are allowed to enjoy and value both their feelings for Isabel and Isabel's feelings – feelings of both maternal and aristocratic excess – which must in the end be rejected. This fracturing of the reader's response replicates the contradictions in mid-Victorian ideologies of motherhood and womanhood.

The Victorian feminine ideal is asexual and passionless, but, at the same time, 'woman' is also the repository of feeling and the source of affectivity. This contradiction is held together by the notion of domestic woman, of whom William Acton wrote, 'love of home, children, and domestic duties, are the only passions they feel'.[55] Moreover, in moral discourse, woman is all spirit (and hence disembodied), and yet in medical discourse she is all body, a body in thrall to its reproductive function. Femininity is defined in terms of renunciation and submission, but these have different meanings when applied to the mother as opposed to the wife: the woman-as-mother sacrifices all for the reproduction of the race; the woman-as-wife sacrifices all for the well-being of the husband. The doctrine of renunciation and submission also leads to moral contradictions, to models of moral conduct which are differently gendered, and to a potential moral enfeeblement of women. John Stuart Mill pointed out some of these problems in *The Subjection of Woman* (1869):

> All the moralities tell them that it is the duty of women, and all the current sentimentalities, that it is their nature, to live for others; to make complete abnegation of themselves, and to have no life but in their affections.[56]

These are some of the conflicts and contradictions from which the drama of *East Lynne* is constructed. They are unified by one thing: the need to control, regulate and manage the feminine feeling that women were taught that they were unable to control for themselves. Women's 'ideal of character', wrote Mill, 'is the very opposite to that of men; not self-will, and government by self-control, but submission, and yielding to the control of others'.[57] *East Lynne* manages these contradictions by means of Wood's own particular combination of sin and sentiment, which involves reworking the conventions of domestic fiction as sensationalized domestic melodrama. Braddon's *Lady Audley's Secret* and *Aurora Floyd* eroticize the female body, and make a spectacle of the racy, assertive woman, or the calculating dangerous woman in domestic disguise. *East Lynne*, on the other hand, eroticizes feminine (womanly) feeling, and makes a spectacle of the sufferings of the female victim. In particular, it makes a spectacle of maternal suffering. In this novel the absent mother is seen, not, from the point of view of the female child's lack of nurture, as it is in so many sensation novels, but rather from the point of view of the needy mother. Maternal deprivation is at the centre of Wood's maternal melodrama. This generic term is more usually applied to film than to novels, but it offers interesting ways of reading *East Lynne*. Maternal melodrama primarily addresses female audiences about issues which mainly concern women. It habitually places its audience within a range of feminine subject positions, and demands the particular 'reading competence' associated with the specific form of feminine subjectivity produced by 'the social fact of female mothering'.[58] In *East Lynne* this positioning is effected by presenting events from Isabel's point of view, or by the very simple device of the confiding, slightly gossipy tone with which the narrator engages the (putative) female reader in a direct woman-to-woman address.

As well as motherhood, domestic life is another of the women's issues which *East Lynne* directly addresses, mainly, although not exclusively, from a woman's point of view. The novel offers two sharply juxtaposed images of women's domestic power: the tyrannical, shrewish old maid, Carlyle's half-sister, Cornelia, and the epitome of modern domestic competence, Barbara Hare/Carlyle. However, the most powerful representations of domestic existence are those which focus on Isabel's predicament: first as the misunderstood and tormented orphan in her aunt's household, then as the wife who is misunderstood by a husband who is preoccupied with his career, and apparently incapable of seeing his wife's isolation and her exclusion from the running of the household by his officious half-sister. (The novel seems to suggest that Carlyle's incomprehension is structural, a function of the male position within the feminine sphere of the home.) Finally, the narrative focuses on Isabel, in her disguise of governess, as the outsider who watches her erstwhile family carrying on with their lives (and deaths), having erased her from the family record. In all of these circumstances Isabel is represented as confined, entrapped, persecuted and suffering within the very space, the home, that was supposed to be both the temple over which women preside and their sanctuary.

Wood's depiction of women's domestic entrapment and subordination directly addresses the actual or potential dissatisfactions of women readers and, at the same time, works to contain and manage those dissatisfactions. No matter how frustrating, hostile or uncomfortable they are, the family and the domestic sphere are represented as essential both for the protection of women, and for the containment of feminine excess. Isabel is most endangered and most dangerous when she is exiled from her home, against her own wishes, for the purposes of convalescence in France. Removed from the protective bosom of her family she is extremely vulnerable to Levison's seductive offensive, and hence becomes a threat to the stability of a society which is based on the control of women's sexuality.

The prolonged 'orgy' of maternal 'self-torture' noted earlier is an important fictional device for managing women's domestic discontents. In the final volume Isabel is persistently represented as the pained and longing spectator of the family she had wilfully deserted, and as the witness of scenes of domestic intimacy between the former husband she now loves and his new wife. Instead of being the source and cause of discontent, the family thus becomes for Isabel, as it does for the reader, an object of desire. The narrator's voice also works to reposition its female readers as domestic creatures. One example must suffice to represent several similar passages to this one which records Isabel's awakening conscience:

> Oh, reader, believe me! Lady – wife – mother! Should you ever be tempted to abandon your home, so will you awake. Whatever trials may be the lot of your married life, though they may magnify themselves to your crushed spirit as beyond the endurance of woman to bear, *resolve* to bear them, fall down upon your knees and pray to be enabled to bear them...bear unto death, rather than forfeit your fair name and your good conscience; for be assured that the alternative if you rush on to it, will be found far worse than death.
>
> Poor...Lady Isabel! She had sacrificed husband, children, reputation, home, all that makes life of value to woman. (*EL* 283)

This address to the reader serves both to reinforce conventional morality, and to 'remind' the woman reader of what she should value most. It also exemplifies the way in which gender ideology is constructed in terms of class concepts. Isabel's suffering, like her sinning, is the product of a class-specific version of sensitively refined femininity, as is emphasized in the continuation of the passage quoted above:

> It is possible remorse does not come to all erring wives so immediately as it came to Lady Isabel Carlyle – you need not be reminded that we speak of women in the higher positions of life. Lady Isabel was endowed with sensitively refined delicacy, with an innate, lively consciousness of right and wrong: a nature such as hers, is one of the last that may be expected to err; and, but for that most fatal misapprehension regarding her husband...she would never have forgotten herself. (*EL* 283–4)

This version of genteel femininity is what makes Isabel both a fallen-woman-as-victim and a heroine – albeit a dead one. The lower-class character Affy Hallijohn, an earlier victim of Isabel's seducer and betrayer, lacks her upper-class refinement and moral scrupulosity, and is, as a consequence, a ridiculed figure rather than a figure of pathos; her fall is associated with her social ambition as well as her sexual and social vulnerability. Between the upper-class victim and the lower-class hardened case stands Barbara Hare, the exemplification of the 'true womanhood' of the bourgeois ideal: a figure whom the reader is asked to admire, but one who does not attract the emotional investment which the reader makes in Isabel.

East Lynne is not simply a warning to wives about the dangers of succumbing to delicious feelings for dashing men, nor is it merely a nightmare vision of the maternal deprivation that will be visited on the mother who strays from her wifely duties. It is also a warning to women against succumbing to certain versions of femininity. If Braddon's *Lady Audley's Secret* and *Aurora Floyd* dramatize respectively the dangers of a manipulative, assertive woman (masquerading as the childlike feminine ideal) and the inadvertently criminal escapades of a boisterous 'Girl of the Period', Wood's apparently more conventional novel shows the dangers of conforming to the feminine ideal. Isabel Vane is precisely the passive, dependent, refined, innocent, childlike woman of the domestic, feminine ideal. It is these characteristics that make her simultaneously and paradoxically both a victim and a villainess. The reader who sees this paradox will see that there are questions to be asked about this ideal, and about the constraints that govern women's lives. There is clearly more than one way to read even the conservative sensation novel.

A different form of maternal melodrama is found in *St Martin's Eve* (1866), the novel in which Wood makes her contribution to the sensation novel's collection of madwomen. If *East Lynne* represents the introverted form of the over-invested mother in Isabel Vane, whose maternal excess is masochistically turned in on herself, then the violent Charlotte Norris (later St John) in *St Martin's Eve* represents maternal excess in demonic, extroverted form. When she becomes a mother Charlotte loves her only son to distraction, and to the exclusion of both her husband and his son and her stepson, Benja.

> The frail little infant [her son Georgy]...had become to her the greatest treasure earth ever gave her; her love for him was of that wild, impassioned, all-absorbing nature, known, it is hoped, but to few, for it never visits a well-regulated heart. (*SME* 39–40)

Or again, following her husband's death:

> One sole passion seemed to absorb her whole life to the exclusion of every other; it filled every crevice of her heart, it regulated her movements, it buried even her natural grief for her husband – and this was the love of her child. The word love is most inadequate to express the feeling: it was as a fiery passion, threatening to consume every healthy impulse. (*SME* 119)

Charlotte's maternal excess is directed against her husband's heir, Benja, in the form of mad, jealous rages and ultimately in her role in his death in a fire. It is hardly to be supposed that the demonic mother should be allowed to get away with this process of unnatural selection. Her own son dies of consumption inherited from his father, and Charlotte is haunted by 'nervous dreams' in which Benja approaches her with a lighted church in his hands before she sinks into a derangement which may be the result of madness inherited from her father, but which is also caused by and figurative of her guilt. Like Lady Audley, Charlotte ends her days in an asylum.

Even when represented in this demonic form, maternal excess and its sufferings contain a weight of sympathy which contradicts the overt moral message of the text. Like Magdalen Vanstone's quasi-criminal scheming in Collins's *No Name*, Charlotte's madness and her violent actions can also be viewed as an extension or perversion of the understandable rage of the woman who is disempowered by her economic dependency, and by a legal system which does not recognize her claims or those of her child. On the other hand, this particular representation of the demonic mother offers a nightmare vision of what women were taught to fear that they might become if they did not submit to the regulation of their passions.

Between the appearance of *East Lynne* and *St Martin's Eve*, Wood published nine other novels: *A Life's Secret* (first serialized anonymously in the Tractarian magazine, *The Leisure Hour*), *The Channings*, *Mrs Halliburton's Troubles*, *The Shadow of Ashlydyat*, *Verner's Pride*, *Oswald Cray*, *Lord Oakburn's Daughters*, *Trevlyn Hold*, and *Mildred Arkell*, most of which are also stories of the control and containment of desire circulating within the family. Wood's narratives represent this process in terms of rivalries within or between families, and between different generations and different social classes. Complicated inheritance plots, often involving lost or altered wills, and irregular or clandestine marriages play an important part in articulating this process. Several of Wood's plots involve a transfer of social power and moral authority from an effete, over-refined or decadent aristocracy (or those who ape aristocratic codes and practices) to the more robust representatives of the yeomanry or bourgeoisie, who are invested with the bourgeois virtues of thrift, hard work and strict conscience.

The moral scrupulosity of the strict conscience, the titillating spectacle of a man and woman of 'refined delicacy thrust by

102

circumstances into extremely indelicate situations',[59] is one of the main sources of sensationalism in Wood's novels. Many critics attribute the sense of moral and social strain, that attends her preoccupation with delicate characters in indelicate situations, to Wood's own social insecurities as the daughter of a provincial glove manufacturer and the wife of a minor shipping agent who was pensioned off because of his mental instability. This may well be the case, but this strain is also an integral part of a moral discourse which is constructed along class lines. The 'strained sufferings' arising from the 'entirely artificial predicaments' and 'exaggerated notions of honour'[60] of Wood's characters, articulate the tortuous (and tortured) process by which socially constructed, gendered subjectivities are produced.

In her dramas of moral scrupulosity, Wood brings together the conventions of popular melodrama and sentimental domestic fiction in a realist mode. The result is neither a simple mixing together of the two forms nor an assimilation of the one by the other. Instead, the two forms exist in what Bakthtin describes as a dialogic relation. In many of Wood's novels (and certainly in *East Lynne)* this dialogue is a destabilizing process, in which the (originally) lower-class form of melodrama subverts, or exists in productive tension with, the forms and norms of the middle-class sentimental novel.

Wood herself both questioned prevailing assumptions about the differences between high and low cultural forms and sought to remove the barriers between them in the pages of the *Argosy*, the literary magazine, which she bought in 1867 and edited until her death in 1887. Wood used this magazine as a vehicle for her own fiction in two ways. It served as a publication outlet for her own brand of domesticated sensation novels, combining sin, sentiment and piety. It was also a platform for the defence of the kind of fiction she wrote. The magazine's unsigned review section, 'Our Log-Book', regularly made the case that good fiction combined realism, sensationalism and sentimentalism and matched interesting characters with a compelling plot, whilst, at the same time, cultivating the sympathies of its readers. In other words, good fiction was what Wood wrote. Like Sala and Braddon in *Belgravia*, Wood's *Argosy* constructed a respectable cultural lineage for the sensation novel. For example, 'Past

Sensationalists' traced a forgotten history of English fiction through the Gothic as exemplified by Monk Lewis's natural supernaturalism and Ann Radcliffe's combination of wild plots and realistic description. Current writers were advised that by blending this past sensationalism with the newer realism they might 'reconcile with greater subtlety the flights of fancy with the facts of real life'.[61] Various *Argosy* essays also sought to argue that 'blending elements of realism and sensationalism' was the most effective way of developing and educating readers' sympathies and changing theirs hearts and minds – something which Wood believed was integral to the social purpose of good fiction. As 'Our Log-Book' put it in September 1860: 'the end of art is not so much to satisfy as to create a noble unrest, in which lies the root of a deeper response'.[62]

OTHER WOMEN SENSATION NOVELISTS

> [N]ovels are more numerous and more highly-coloured than they used to be, and these numerous and highly-coloured novels are chiefly composed by women.[63]

Mary Elizabeth Braddon and Ellen Wood were by no means the first nineteenth-century women writers to be labelled as sensation novelists and nor were they the last. For example, Margaret Oliphant claimed that the model for the female novelists' sensation heroine was Jane Eyre in Charlotte Brontë's novel of 1847, and her spirited 1867 attack on sensation fiction's misrepresentation of 'how young women of good blood and training feel'[64] was directed at Annie Thomas, Rhoda Broughton and the 'very nasty books' of Ouida, as well as at Braddon. Annie Thomas was also included in 'the Ladies' Fast-Life Literary Academy', described in the *Broadway* article quoted at the beginning of this chapter and section, 'a class of female novelists who depict the peccadilloes of fictitious fashionable life rather than its crimes, and who write as a fast young lady in a garrison town might be supposed to write while aping the character of a fast young man'.[65] The *Broadway* also included Ouida in this class of female novelists along with Annie Edwards and Florence Marryat. The final section of this chapter refers briefly to the works of these five novelists.

Annie Thomas, whose *Played Out* (1866) and *Called to Account* (1867), were singled out for adverse comment by Margaret Oliphant in her 1867 attack on sensation fiction in the September issue of *Blackwood's*, had a long and prolific career as the author of over seventy novels as well as stories and sketches which she published in such magazines as *St Paul's*, *Temple Bar*, and *All the Year Round*. Her main fictional subjects in the 1860s were fallen women, the faults of men, marriage and divorce, domesticity and motherhood. The *Broadway* dismissed her novels as lacking in real life but containing 'a great deal of "Bell's Life"' (a weekly sporting paper), as her male characters 'smoke, drink, and swear inordinately, and talk unceasing slang'. In general her characters were said to be 'ill-behaved, disreputable people' who are enveloped in an 'atmosphere of distrust', with husbands and wives 'watch[ing] each other furtively when the postman arrives, for there is sure to be some compromising missive in the letter-bag'.[66] Oliphant was particularly scathing about Thomas's use of a sensation device, 'which is becoming about as general as the golden hair': this is the device (described by Oliphant as 'a poor expedient') of casting doubt on the heroine's reputation by engineering an innocent chance situation in which she spends the night with a man with whom she has previously been known to flirt. Although Thomas has the sensation novelist's flair for telling a good story (as Oliphant concedes), she remains, for the most part, one of those forgotten writers of the nineteenth century whose works go largely unread. Perhaps, as Andrew Maunder has recently suggested, she is one of the forgotten female sensationalists who is due for reassessment.[67]

Another candidate for reassessment is Annie Edwards (who later adopted the spelling Edwardes), another prolific author who began her career by producing books of the 'sensational and rapid school'.[68] *The Morals of May Fair* (1858) was followed by numerous books with racy titles and subjects, including *The World's Verdict* (1860), *The Ordeal for Wives; A Story of London Life* (1864), *Ought We to Visit Her?* (1871), *A Vagabond Heroine* (1873), and *Leah, A Woman of Fashion* (1874). Edwards's novels and her writing career demonstrate some of the thematic continuities between the sensation novel and the New Woman fiction of the end of the nineteenth century. Her later novels, which often focused on 'New Woman' characters, included *A Bluestocking* (1877) and *A Girton Girl* (1885).

Florence Marryat, another of the *Broadway's* 'fast' lady-novelists, was one of the authors to whom Elaine Showalter referred, in *A Literature of Their Own*, when she sought to demonstrate how the women's sensation novel was a 'genuinely radical protest against marriage and women's economic oppression in the framework of feminine conventions that demanded the erring heroine's destruction'.[69] Marryat, who published over seventy-five novels, began her career with a bang in 1865, with three novels appearing in that year: *Love's Conflict* (January), *Too Good for Him* (May) and *Woman Against Woman* (issued December, dated 1866). A firm believer that women should lead independent working lives, this twice-married, once-divorced and once-separated writer went on to create a number of strong-minded, independent heroines who earned their own living, for example, as actresses, writers, teachers and nurses. However, Elfrida Salisbury, the heroine of Marryat's first novel, *Love's Conflict*, moves directly from school to marriage and her 'Struggle for Life' (to quote the novel's working title) is the struggle of a wife. Elfrida begins the narrative as a 'mad, laughter-loving girl, whose wildness had been the cause of many a grave reproof... from governesses' (*LC* 150), and ends it as a compliant and dutiful wife who has learned to love her husband some years after their marriage. Like Aurora Floyd, the eighteen-year-old Elfrida encountered at the outset of Marryat's narrative is both venturesome and inexperienced and lacks a mother's guiding hand. She and her sister Grace have spent most of their lives in England, while their parents remained in India where her father was a doctor in the Indian Civil Service and her mother's premature death subsequently removes an important support at a crucial stage of Elfrida's life. However, far from marrying beneath her in a fit of sensual passion (to paraphrase Oliphant's description of the actions of Aurora and other sensation heroines), the 'wild' Elfrida is tricked into an engagement with the well-to-do William Treherne, a selfish, unprincipled man with whom she has had a fleeting flirtation, when he deliberately engineers her into a compromising situation during her voyage out to India to join her parents. Having married William in full knowledge that she does not

106

love him – 'looking like a martyr in her wedding garments' (*LC* 150) – Elfrida subsequently becomes the focus of Marryat's presentation of the spectacle of the sufferings and temptations of a vulnerable young woman trapped in a marriage to a neglectful husband who shares none of his wife's tastes. The stage is set for the adultery plot that is one of the staples of sensation fiction. In this case George Treherne, who had never before met a woman who meets his exacting standards, falls in love with his cousin William's wife and she with him. Much of the second volume focuses on George and Elfrida's grappling with their feelings for each other until a sensation scene in which George seeks to persuade Elfrida to go away with him. Unlike Wood's Isabel Vane, Elfrida, who is pregnant with her husband's child, does not succumb to temptation, but to a nervous illness. An adulteress in thought if not in fact, Elfrida reaps the harvest of her putative sin in a variation of Wood's maternal melodrama. In this novel the reader is offered a spectacle of maternal suffering in which Elfrida, having repeatedly bemoaned the fact of her pregnancy, gives birth to a 'deformed' son:

> She looked in silence, long and deep silence, at every part of the little crippled frame. Then she bent over and kissed, with a reverent tenderness, the tiny deformed limbs, kissed them softly, and yet with a passion, apparent in her eyes. (*LC* 291)

Her son survives only a few hours and is intensely mourned by his mother, who interprets his death as God's punishment for her illicit love for George. Elfrida also blames her passionate exchanges with George for the child's deformities, which her doctor attributes to 'a serious shock of mind or body' (*LC* 288).

Elfrida's maternal melodrama lays the ground for another variant of the sensation plot in which she learns to love and become a dutiful wife to the man with whom she had made a loveless marriage. In this case the transformation is effected when she returns to the husband, who cast her out following her confession of her illicit love for his cousin, and nurses him back to health after an illness which had caused him to reassess both his life and his wife – and his earlier treatment of her. The novel's ending smacks of the sin and sentiment favoured by Wood. The woman who began the novel as a wild child ends it as a dutiful wife and woman of two loves:

> Her happiness is a true happiness, because it proceeds from doing her duty. Her love for her husband is a true love, arising from gratitude for his trust in her; but the other love was a part of her life, and while she exists it cannot die. And why not? Because the consequences of our actions remain with us, long after the actions are...done with. We may strive to soften their effect upon others...but it is not so easy to snip out the remembrance of them for ourselves. Our hearts are sensitive, our memories are keen, and life is too short for forgetfulness. (*LC* 420)

Despite its focus on the heroine's illicit love for a man who is not her husband, Marryat's novel could hardly be said to provide that sensuous dwelling on the physicality of women's sexual feelings for which sensation fiction was often criticized. To be sure Elfrida's body is displayed for the reader, as is the fulsome body of Hélène Brossart, whom George marries following his rejection by Elfrida, and who features in the novel's inheritance and attempted blackmail plots, and in a sensational murder scene. However, Marryat is much more concerned to depict Elfrida's nervousness, her tendency to succumb to feverish illnesses and, in the depths of her travails, to take an anorexic's pleasure in the wasting away of her body, than she is to portray her taking pleasure in the contemplation of male muscles. Similarly, despite Hélène's youthful dalliance with a lower-class man and the fact that she is the daughter of a fallen woman (a daughter of the Treherne family who had run away with her French music teacher), she is presented as glorying in her power over the feelings of men, rather than having strong sexual feelings of her own. *Love's Conflict* does, however, display the sensation novel's interest in matters sexual. Indeed, one of its more remarkable features is the frankness of its treatment of the sexual double standard. Hélène's mother is exiled from her family and set on the slippery slope to life as a fallen woman as a result of a youthful sexual adventure. On the other hand William Treherne's reputation for sexual exploits does not prevent his acceptance as a suitable husband for an innocent girl who is little more than a child. Moreover, the novel is particularly explicit about the sexual debauchery in which both William and George indulge, when the former discovers the truth about his wife's feelings for George and the latter fails to persuade her to go away with him. However, Marryat's dwelling on the details of their behaviour is compensated for by her depiction of the way in which William's customary pleasure in debauchery is spoiled by his recollection of Elfrida's purity – a recollection which similarly increases George's self-loathing.

Like other sensation novels, *Love's Conflict* is modern and up-to-date. Set in the 1850s, with references to the Indian Mutiny of 1857–8, the novel in part traces the movement of power, energy and worth from a moribund feudal class to a new professional class. Both William and George have spent their lives waiting to come into their inheritance, but neither of them really knows what to do with it. Even without the disappointment in love (and the cynicism of his subsequent marriage) which tarnishes George's coming into possession of his uncle's estate of Ariscedwyn, his experience as a professional soldier has unfitted him for a life of hunting, shooting and directing others to manage the estate: he 'must have *work*', 'anything to be useful…my head and my hands are at the world's service' (*LC* 371). Among the novel's male characters the most measured and morally worthy are those who are seriously engaged in their professions: the soldier, Charles Digby, and the doctors, Salis-bury and Cameron.

Love's Conflict was widely reviewed as a disturbing and dangerous book, although, unlike many sensation novels it was praised for the quality of the writing. In the second half of the 1860s Marryat continued to supply the sensation market with tales of murder, madness, seduction, mercenary marriages, extra-marital liaisons, adultery and bigamy among the middle and upper classes – with some excursions into the *demi-monde* – in novels such as *Woman Against Woman* (1865), *Too Good for Him* (1865), *The Confessions of Gerald Estcourt* (1867), *Nelly Brooke* (1868), *Veronique* (1868) and *The Girls of Feversham* (1869). Like Braddon and Wood, Marryat also became the 'conductor' of a magazine, which she used as a vehicle for her own fiction. From 1872–6 she edited *London Society*, an illustrated monthly magazine aimed at the middle and upper classes. In the late 1870s she also branched out into a second career as an actress and writer for the theatre.

Ouida was another member of the school of 'fast lady-novelists' with a penchant for tales about soldiers, whose novels enjoyed sensational sales in the 1860s. She was initially reviewed as a sensation novelist by Oliphant, partly because of timing: her first novel *Granville de Vigne: A Tale of the Day* (which appeared in volume form as *Held in Bondage* in 1863) began its serial run in the *New Monthly Magazine* in January 1861, alongside the final instalments of Wood's *East Lynne*, which had begun its serialization a year earlier. Moreover, both *Held in Bondage* and her next novel, *Strathmore* (1863–5), are melodramatic love stories which contain many of the stock ingredients of the sensation novel: secrecy, bigamy, adultery, murder, and characters erroneously assumed to be dead. Like many sensation fictions Ouida's novels also disrupt or blur conventional gender stereotypes with their representation of strong, active, female characters and male characters who have both masculine and feminine characteristics. Examples of this cross-gendering include: the bigamous adventuress Lucy Davis (also known as Constance Trefusis) in *Held in Bondage*, whose 'tall and voluptuously perfect figure'[70] is presented to the reader's gaze in the manner of the sensation heroine/villainess; the fiery, intelligent and resourceful Alma Tresillian, in the same novel, who speaks up in defence of women's 'passions, ambitions, impatience at their own monotonous role' (vol. 2, 58) and breaks out from the bondage into which de Vigne has entrapped her; the self-worshipping Marion Marchioness of Vavasour and Vaux in *Strathmore*, who uses her beauty as a weapon of power and control; Cigarette in *Under Two Flags*, who wears the uniform of a *vivandière* in the French Foreign Legion and swears, smokes, drinks and gambles like a trooper, yet 'was not wholly unsexed...and had not left a certain feminine grace behind her';[71] Arthur Chevasney, the feminized dandy who narrates *Held in Bondage* and his idol Granville de Vigne, who combines the muscularity of a gladiator or Greek statue with a feminine slightness of form and delicate lips; Strathmore, the eponymous hero of Ouida's second novel, a forcefully masculine yet dandified character and his best friend Bertie Erroll, the *Beau Sabreur*, 'the solitary person whom Strathmore could ever have been said to have loved',[72] who is described as being 'Gentle as a woman and as lazy as a Circassian girl (vol.1, 8); Bertie, the Beauty of the Guards, the hero of Ouida's best-seller, *Under Two Flags* (1867), who begins the novel as a dandified libertine, whose face is described as having 'as much delicacy and brilliancy as a woman's' and whose 'features were exceedingly fair – fair as the fairest girl's' (vol. 1, 4).

Much of Ouida's fiction also shares the sensation novel's concern with marriage and divorce. The attack on the marriage market offered by Violet Molyneux, in *Held in Bondage* is not untypical of Ouida's representation of marriage as legal prostitution:

> Marriage is the mart, mothers the auctioneers, and he who bids the highest wins...I consider a marriage de convenance the most gross of all social falsehood. You prostitute the most sacred vows and outrage the closest social ties; you carry a lie to your husband's heart and home...The Quadroon girl sold in the slave-market is not so utterly polluted as the woman free, educated, and enlightened, who barters herself, for a 'marriage for position'. (vol.3, 88)

Like many sensation novels Ouida's novels of fashionable life tend to portray marriage as a state of entrapment and confinement for both men and women. However, Ouida's 'fast' novels are rather more open about the extent to which the worldly escape the limitations of marriage by engaging in more or less discreet adulterous liaisons, and/or by resort to the divorce courts. For example, *Held in Bondage*, which began its serial publication only four years after the passage of the 1857 Matrimonial Causes Act, has some of its characters debate the current state of the divorce laws, which provided such a rich seam of plots for sensation fiction:

> If you divorce for insanity, every husband sick of his wife can get a certificate of lunacy against her. If for drunkenness, what woman will be safe from having drams innumerable sworn against her?...At the same time divorce seems...of all the niceties of legislature, the most ticklish and unsatisfactory to adjust....to shut the door on divorce...is an evil unbearable;...open it too wide, almost as much harm may accrue. (vol.1, 242)

By the time that *Under Two Flags* appeared, some ten years after the passing of the 1857 Divorce Act, some of Ouida's characters are more blasé about the subject; as one of the fashionable young men in this novel remarks, 'everybody goes through the DC [Divorce Court] somehow or other...It's like the Church, the Commons and the Gallows, you know – one of the popular institutions' (vol. 1, 132).

As well as sharing the sensation novel's concern with the commodification of marriage and relations between the sexes, Ouida's early fiction also shares its preoccupation with the material aspects of middle and upper-class life. Like Braddon's early sensation novels, Ouida's fiction displays the luxurious trappings of the homes of upper and upper middle-class characters, in ways which appealed to the aspirations and consumerism of her middle-class readers and, at the same time, offered a critique of the emptiness or vulgarity of such materialism. In keeping with her disruption of conventional gender stereotypes, in Ouida's novels the luxurious boudoir is as likely to belong to a male as to a female character. For example the dressing-room of Bertie, the Beauty of the Guards, in *Under Two Flags* is a masculine (or, perhaps, cross-gendered) version of the luxurious feminine disorder of Lady Audley's boudoir:

> The dressing case was of silver, with the name studded in the lid in turquoises; the brushes, bootjacks, boot trees, whip-stands, were of ivory and tortoise shell.... The hangings of the room were silken and rose-coloured, and a delicious confusion prevailed through it pell-mell, box-spurs, hunting-stirrups, cartridge-cases...mixed up with Paris novels, pink notes, point-lace ties, bracelets and bouquets. (vol.1, 3)

The splendour of Bertie's dressing-room and Lady Audley's boudoir are equally illusory: in his case it is based on debt and in hers deception.

Ouida's exotic love stories were regarded as sensational by some early reviewers because of their frank depiction of sexuality and the sexual mores of their high society settings. One of the other main targets of perhaps the most concerted attack on the innocent indecency (to paraphrase Oliphant) of the sensation novel was Rhoda Broughton's first published novel *Cometh Up As A Flower*, which bore the brunt of Oliphant's rage in her September 1867 article in *Blackwood's* – in which she misidentified the novel's author as Annie Thomas. Oliphant regarded both the story and the mode of telling it as sensational. It is the story of two motherless sisters: the irreverent, rebellious, childlike heroine Nell Lestrange, who falls in love with a dashing but penniless dragoon Dick M'Gregor; and her older sister Dolly, whose conventional beauty and polished social veneer masks cynicism, duplicity and deceit. Dolly, 'cold blooded, mercenary, revengeful, hesitating at nothing which will further her ends',[73] forges a letter in order to part the young lovers and ensure that Nell rescues the family from financial ruin by marrying an older and wealthy baronet, Sir Hugh Lancaster, whom she finds physically repulsive. After her marriage Nell continues to pine for Dick and, having discovered her sister's machinations, she offers to leave her husband to go away with him – an offer which Dick honourably declines. Nell goes into a decline and abandons a plan to expose her sister's deception and ruin her chances of an advantageous marriage to Lord Stockport. The sensationalism of the plot was heightened by the fact that its narrator was the 'free-spoken heroine',[74] who confides her story with disarming or alarming candour, depending on one's point of view. Oliphant found the narrator-heroine's clear-eyed view of the nature of her marital situation, and the frank tones in which she described it, particularly shocking. Others might have found it too near the mark for comfort when the heroine describes her marriage as, 'the most matter-of-fact piece of barter in the world; so much young flesh for so much current coin of the realm' (CUF 260), or when she narrates her sensations of repulsion at her husband's touch:

> His arm is around my waist and he is brushing my eyes and cheeks...with his somewhat bristly moustache as often as he feels inclined – for am I not his property...for has he not bought me...for so many pounds of prime white flesh, he has paid down handsomely on the nail...that accursed, girdling arm is still round me – my buyer's arm – that arm which seems to be burning into my flesh like a brand. (CUF 269)

Or again, Nell's frank admission that:

> I had indulged a mild, vague hope that the very words of the marriage ceremony read over me would have a cabalistic charm to prevent my ever thinking of any man but Sir Hugh, after we were man and wife. I had heard that only very bad wicked women ever cared for anybody but their husbands after they were married, and I hoped that I was not a very bad wicked woman.
>
> However, I had discovered pretty soon with some chagrin that I must reckon myself among that naughty band...I found that I thought of Dick infinitely more; more regretfully, passionately, longingly, now that I was Lady Lancaster, and it was criminal of me

so to think, than I had done as Nelly Lestrange, when it was only unwise and unworldly. (*CUF* 292)

Broughton's novel, seen by Oliphant as a 'sample of the kind of expression given by modern fiction to modern sentiments from a woman's point of view',[75] was thought to be particularly disgusting when the heroine dwelt on her longing for physical contact with her soldier lover and her loathing for the touch of her husband. Geraldine Jewsbury, whose review in the *Athenaeum* assumed the novel to be the work of a man, deplored its 'free and unrestrained utterance' and 'all pervading coarseness of thought and expression'.[76] However, for all the critical focus on the portrayal of the heroine's sensations and bodily passions, the novel ends with the wasting away of the body as Nell declines into an early death from consumption. The ironic distance with which Nell narrates this aspect of her story is typical of the witty fictional self-consciousness of this novel:

> I am buried in an arm-chair in my boudoir, reading a novel about a married woman, who ran away from her husband and suffered the extremity of human ills in consequence. I have made several steps in morality of late I flatter myself, but even now, I can hardly imagine that I should have been very miserable if Dick had taken me away with him.... The naughty matron is just dying of a broken heart and starvation in a Penitentiary, when I hear carriage wheels...(*CUF* 313–4)

This is typical of what Tamar Heller describes as this novel's 'extravagant pastiche of allusions to earlier literary works and conventional ways of telling women's stories' by means of which Broughton foregrounds 'the generic instability of her own narrative of female desire'.[77]

The instabilities and contradictions of female desire are also the subject of *Not Wisely But Too Well*,[78] the second of Broughton's novels to appear in volume form but written and serialized before the success of *Cometh Up As A Flower*. *Not Wisely* is the story of another witty and passionate young heroine, Kate Chester, who falls passionately in love with an unprincipled aristocrat, Dare Stamer, with whom she prepares to elope before discovering that he is married. Recovering from the brain fever to which she succumbs as a result of the frustration of her continuing passion for Stamer, Kate immerses herself in charitable work under the guidance of a saintly young clergyman, James Stanley, whom she nurses during his fatal illness. The narrative concludes with Kate's melodramatic reunion with Stamer as he is dying from injuries received in a carriage accident, and her subsequent decision to become an Anglican Sister of Mercy; in the more sensational serial version Stamer shoots both Kate and himself on the night before she enters a convent. In the reader's report in which she recommended that Bentley's reject *Not Wisely*, Geraldine Jewsbury described it as 'the most thoroughly sensuous tale I have read in English for a long time'.[79] However, despite being targeted as one of the main perpetrators of the sensation novel's 'intense appreciation of flesh and blood' and 'eagerness of physical sensation',[80] Broughton, in this novel as in its predecessor, focuses on the pains as well as pleasures of female desire. Like Nell Lestrange, Kate Chester also declines from her original ruddy roundness – Kate's body is described as having the 'ripe womanly development of one of Titian's Venuses'[81] – into a more spectral figure. Moreover, although both narrowly avoid the sexual slavery of the mistress and the role of ruined woman towards which their passions and sexual appetites propel them, they are portrayed as enslaved by their passions and the men with whom they are infatuated.

Despite the mixed critical reception for her debut novels Broughton, unlike the heroine of her 1894 novel *A Beginner*, was not deterred from pursuing a career as a novelist. In all she published twenty-six novels, the last appearing posthumously shortly after her death in 1920. However, compared with her first two tales of spirited young women possessing as the *Spectator's* reviewer put it, 'an exuberant mental life' and 'despising conventionality and contemning the usual cut-and-dried formulas for living',[82] her later novels tended to be more conventional courtship novels with heroines who were less sexually daring. Nevertheless Broughton continued to rework some sensation elements: the heroine with a secret (a concealed engagement) in *Red As A Rose Is She* (1870), or the suspected adultery plot in a tale of an initially loveless marriage of a young woman and a much older man in *Nancy* (1873), and a continuing focus on the economics of marriage and the limited economic opportunities for unmarried women.

4

Aftershocks: The Sensation Legacy

SENSATIONALISM IN NINETEENTH-CENTURY FICTION

Just as the phenomenon of sensationalism existed before the term entered general usage in the 1860s, sensation conventions and plots continued their existence long after the sensation boom of the 1860s had passed. The tentacles of sensationalism spread widely into many different kinds of fiction in the mid-Victorian period, extending their reach into a number of fictional developments at the end of the century. Whether or not they were labelled as sensation novelists, most novelists of the 1850s and 1860s – and beyond – worked with the same complex multiple plots as the sensation novelists and, like them, engaged in the process of defining, reworking and redefining realism. They were also concerned with similar issues: class, social change, sex, money, family, morals, manners and marriage and its alternatives. In short, sensation plots, sensation types, sensation themes, and sensation machinery were integral parts of the storehouse of conventions from which all Victorian novelists drew.

The appropriation and revision of melodrama which was such a significant feature of sensation fiction was also undertaken by numerous other nineteenth-century novelists from Dickens to Hardy. Indeed, several nineteenth-century reviewers and critics regarded Dickens as the founder of the 'sensation school'. Certainly Dickens shared the sensation novelists' interest in crime and criminals, and novels such as *Dombey and Son* (1846–8) and *Bleak House* (1852–3) anticipated the sensation novel's concern with women with secret, problematic marriages, adultery and irregular sexual liaisons. In *Bleak House* Dickens also made use of the detective as the hunter out of the secrets of women and the family and the evils of society. *Great Expectations*, which was reviewed alongside *The Woman in White*, has many sensation elements, including white collar crime and men and women with secret histories. Moreover, like many sensation novels, it contrives to suggest that respectable society both conceals and is supported by a dark, criminal under-life. Like Collins, Braddon and Wood, Dickens is what Peter Brooks calls a 'social melodramatist'.[1] His is a serious reworking of the forms of melodrama, which strives 'to articulate, to demonstrate, to "prove" the existence of a moral universe which, though put into question, masked by villainy and perversions of judgement, does exist'.[2]

If Dickens was a serious sensationalist, Anthony Trollope was one of the many novelists who parodied the excesses of sensation fiction. *The Eustace Diamonds* (serialized in the *Fortnightly Review* between July 1871 and February 1873) parodically rewrites *The Moonstone* by constructing a plot around a vulgar, socially ambitious young woman who steals her own diamonds, as Cuff had erroneously suspected Collins's Rachel Verinder of doing. Elsewhere, however, Trollope occupies the terrain of the sensation novel on its own terms. *Orley Farm*, for example, centres on the familiar sensation situations of the lady of high social rank and moral reputation who has a dark secret in her past, as well as the complications arising from confusions over wills and codicils. The basic sensation ingredients of crime, violence and sexual scandal regularly formed part of the social and political novels of this writer, who thought that a good novel should be 'at the same time realistic and sensational'.[3]

George Meredith, an early example of a self-consciously 'high-brow' novelist and an influential figure in nineteenth-century publishing through his role as a reader for the publishers Chapman and Hall, deplored the melodramatic plots and (what he saw as) unrealistic characters of Collins and other sensationalists. Nevertheless, even he did not avoid the use of the preoccupations and plot devices of the sensation novel. At the beginning of his career, as Benjamin Fisher has noted, Meredith 'emulated Collins's sensationalism' in novels such as *Evan Harrington* (1861), by undertaking 'some deft inversions of

Collins's materials in *The Dead Secret* to serve his own idea of greater depths in psychological portraiture'.[4] By the mid-1860s Meredith bowed to the pressure of the literary marketplace in his efforts to widen his readership and increase the income he earned from his novel writing. In *Rhoda Fleming* (1865), as Sally Mitchell has noted, Meredith offered readers a 'plain story' about an unchaste woman in which 'virtually every element of character and situation might be duplicated in any number of novels from the early 1860s':

> the farmer's daughter drawn to the city by her search for excitement, the son of a baronet-banker who abandons her because of class and family, the widowed adventuress over whom two duels have been fought, the bigamist who ships his wife off to America so he can marry for money, the misappropriated funds and intercepted letters.[5]

George Eliot attacked the silly novels by lady novelists of the generation before she began writing fiction, but made much use of the conventions of those sensational lady novelists whose heyday coincided with the early years of her own career. Eliot often deployed sensation effects and sensation machinery in her attempts to render the moral universe legible, and to develop a form of realism in which she could conduct her 'experiments in life' which endeavoured to see 'what our thought and emotion may be capable of'.[6] *Felix Holt the Radical* (1866), published just after the height of the sensation boom, bears many of the hallmarks of the sensation novel. At the centre of the plot is Mrs Transome, an imperious woman with a taste for 'dangerous French authors', who radiates repressed passion and 'bitter discontent'. She is also a woman with a secret, which involves a past adulterous affair and its continuing results. Mrs Transome's secret functions in the same way as the secrets in sensation novels: a cross-class, illicit sexual liaison undermines the upper classes, puts them in the power of their social inferiors, and disrupts the stability and continuity of the family and its property. The similarities between George Eliot and her sensational sisters did not go unremarked by reviewers. The *Contemporary Review* described 'Lady Audley and Mrs Transome ...[as] true twin sisters of fiction', and accused Eliot of joining hands with Braddon in reversing 'the grand old idea of ... heroic behaviour, by cunningly eliciting our sympathy for individuals placed in doubtful circumstances, who fall into falsely tragical positions because of their weaknesses'.[7]

Even *Middlemarch* (1871–2), the archetypal novel of high Victorian realism and moral seriousness, is not without sensation elements. The Dorothea, Casaubon, Ladislaw triangle is a sort of shadow adultery/bigamy plot often found in sensation novels, as is the relationship of Rosamund with Lydgate and Ladislaw. The seemingly respectable banker, Bulstrode, has the obligatory secret skeleton in his past, and Raffles turns up as if from a sensation novel to provide the necessary plot machinery to expose it. Eliot's final novel, *Daniel Deronda* (1876), also has many sensational features: 'tangled and intricate intrigue', 'lost fathers and unknown mothers', 'melo-dramatic confrontations', 'mysterious past passions', illegitimate children and other 'skeletons in cupboards'.[8] It also has, in common with *The Moonstone*, the not-quite-wife and family in the villa who, in this case, emerge from their concealment to confront the heroine with an unpleasant truth about the man she is about to marry. However, the most remarkable aspect of this novel's sensationalism is its development of the 'actual psychology of sensation' in its dramatization of Gwendolen's irrational fears and its exploration of her 'nervous equipment'.[9] Gwendolen's moral character is articulated in terms of her nervous sensations (which the reader is also made to feel), and her moral development begins in sensations of fear and terror.

Thomas Hardy's first novel, the anonymously published *Desperate Remedies* (1871), was an example of sensationalism run riot. It was, as Hardy later wrote in the Preface to the novel, a 'long and intricately inwrought chain of circumstance'[10] involving murder, blackmail, illegitimacy, impersonation, eaves-dropping, multiple secrets, a suggestion of bigamy, amateur and professional detectives. Although Hardy was later to dismiss his early novel (in a Prefatory note added in August 1912) as 'this sensational and strictly conventional narrative', sensational and melodramatic modes and concerns continued to be an im-portant part of his fiction.[11] They are evident in the rhetorical excess of his style, particularly in his representation of female characters: the Braddonesque 'Queen of the Night' passage on Eustacia Vye in *The Return of the Native* (which first appeared in

119

Belgravia, a magazine noted for its sensational fiction, in 1878), and the anatomizing of Tess Durbeyfield in *Tess of the D'Urbervilles* (1891) come immediately to mind. Sensationalism is also present in Hardy's heavy reliance on coincidence, and in the way in which his plots are habitually structured by the secrets of the past returning to shape the present and future lives of his characters. Hardy's sensational antecedents can also be seen in his treatment of the 'deadly war waged between flesh and spirit',[12] and in his persistent focus on troubled marriages and the problematic nature of marriage as an institution.

Hardy's representation of a deterministic, Darwinian universe in which the characteristic experiences are suffering, anxiety, and frustrated aims continues the revision of the conventions and moral vision of the popular melodrama which was begun by the novelists of the 1860s. For the sensation novelists, as for several of the other fiction writers discussed above, and especially for Hardy, the abstract struggle between moral absolutes which was staged in the popular melodrama became a much more historically and socially particularized set of struggles, played out in a fragmented world in which the boundaries between moral categories were increasingly blurred and relativized. In the sensation fiction of the 1860s, the happy ending of marriage and an integrated social life and/or the final triumph of bourgeois virtue remained a possibility, and it was regularly pulled out of the top hat in order to reassure readers whose moral universe and social convictions were so effectively disturbed by other aspects of the sensation plot. The resolution of the sensation plot is often achieved against the grain of both the narrative and moral puzzles around which it is constructed, and readers are left with the uneasy feeling that the supposedly civilized social surfaces of the age of materialism and progress are neither as civilized nor as natural as they were supposed to be.

Although sensation elements were deeply embedded in Victorian fiction, the boom in the sensation novel was a phenomenon of the 1860s, and several critics were eager to pronounce its demise well before the end of that decade. Nevertheless, 'sensation novel' proved a remarkably resilient term in both the marketing and reviewing of fiction into the 1890s, and regularly cropped up in advertisements for new and reissued fiction. For example, in 1883, the *Belfast News-Letter* was just one of a number of regional British papers to carry an advertisement for the recently issued cheap edition of Mrs Southgate's *Out of the Depths or the Struggles of a Gallant Life* as 'THE GREAT SENSATION NOVEL OF REAL LIFE', offering 'startling situations; mystery sustained; plots well developed and... high moral purpose and healthy sentiment dominating the whole work',[13] and in the same year an advertisement for Fanny M. Gallagher's *Thy Name is Truth: a Social Novel*, quotes the *Athenaeum's* review describing it as 'a clever specimen of a sensation novel'.[14] In 1884 the *Sheffield and Rotherham Independent* (among other newspapers) ran an advertisement for *Wyllard's Weird* 'A NEW AND EXCITING SENSATION NOVEL BY MISS BRADDON'.[15]

As well as being used as a marketing label in advertisements, the term 'sensation novel' continued to be used in reviews in periodicals, newspapers and popular magazines through the 1880s, and, a little less frequently, right up until the end of the nineteenth century.[16] It was most often used as a shorthand term, a convenient descriptor to signal to those who liked, among other things, startling situations, sustained mystery and well developed plots that the book under review was one that might suit them, or that they should avoid it as an indifferent example of this kind of fiction. Alternatively, it was a warning that the novel should be avoided by those who disliked sensation fiction in general. Examples of this kind of usage include a review of Charles Quentin's *Through the Storm* (1880) in the *Graphic*, as 'one of the worst specimens of a sensation novel it has been our misfortune to meet for sometime',[17] and the *Standard's* review of Frank Barrett's *Under a Strange Mask* (1889), describing it as 'a sensation novel in the best sense of the word'.[18] An interesting snippet in the *Morning Post's* 'Book of the Day' for June 6 1895 noted that Richard Penderel's *A Fleet Street Journalist* has come to the rescue of the lover of sensation novels:

> those whose favourite fiction is of the sensational kind have been kept on short commons for a good many years past... Sensation fiction there has been no doubt... but it has, as a rule, taken an unwholesome form, and for the delights of the original sensation novel, the reader who loved them of old has often pined in vain, thankful for such morsels [provided by] J. Clark Russell... Conan

Doyle, or...Frankfort Moore, but fretting at the pauper fare provided by writers who appear to regard one or two dastardly crimes, a single struggle for life, and a mysterious disappearance as a sufficient supply of the purely sensational element in a work of moderate proportions'.[19]

As late as October 1897 *Hearth and Home* was reviewing Violet Hunt's *Unkist, Unkind* as a technically good example of the sensation novel, while noting that 'the sensation novel is scarcely her forte'.[20]

While there can be no doubt that novels were being marketed and reviewed as sensation novels well beyond the 1860s and also that the term 'sensation' continued to be a point of reference for reviewers and for commentators on the state of fiction well into the 1890s, by the late 1880s it is not always clear that the term 'sensation novel' refers to the same kind of book as it did in the 1860s. For example, when *The Standard* launched into an assessment of the current state of fiction in February 1887 in its report of a recent Toynbee Hall lecture given by H. D. Traill, it opines that alongside the revival of romance and the tale of the supernatural by Robert Louis Stevenson, Rider Haggard, F. Anstey, Hugh Conway and Marion Crawford, '[o]ther novelists again have contented themselves with creating "strong" plots and effective situations, without trespassing on the supernatural or the fantastic', and notes that 'the "sensation" novel is once more recognized as work which is worthy the attention of literary men – and women – of knowledge, culture and established reputation'.[21] *The Standard* neglects to say who these other novelists are, but in November 1887 the *Derby Mercury* reveals that a 'new sensation novel-writer has sprung up amongst us who is content to be known to the world as "Q"', and notes that 'his [Arthur Quiller Couch's] first work, "Dead Man's Rock" [is] a good, honest, nerve-trying, back-creeping novel'.[22]

These last two reviews remind us that the late-nineteenth-century sensation legacy includes the *fin-de-siècle* revival of romance and tales of the fantastic, which, like the sensation novel, represent a range of responses to technological modernity and the accompanying modernization of the senses.[23] Such narratives include Robert Louis Stevenson's *The Strange Case of Dr Jekyll and Mr Hyde* (1886), Rider Haggard's *She* (1887), Oscar Wilde's *The Picture of Dorian Gray* (1891), Arthur Machen's *The*

Great God Pan (1894), Bram Stoker's *Dracula* (1897) and Mary Elizabeth Braddon's vampire narrative 'Good Lady Ducayne' (1896), and also H.G. Wells's scientific romances – *The Time Machine* (1895), *The Island of Doctor Moreau* (1896), *The Invisible Man* (1897), *The War of the Worlds* (1898), *When the Sleeper Wakes* (1899) and *The First Men in the Moon* (1901). As I have noted elsewhere, one important link between the sensation novel and its mutations in *fin-de-siècle* romance and fantastic fiction is a narrative complicatedness, manifested in the widespread use of layered, framed, and embedded narratives including journal extracts and other ostensible documentary records. Such devices work both to create an illusion of verisimilitude and to disperse narrative authority, disrupt narrative causality and problematize origins.[24]

Narrative complicatedness and intricately constructed plots also connect the sensation novel to later nineteenth-century developments in detective fiction. Mrs Oliphant's prediction, in her review of Collins's *The Woman in White*, that 'it is into the hands of the literary Detective that this school of story-telling must fall at last',[25] proved to be prescient. Like Oliphant, other leading fiction reviewers in the 1860s tended to castigate the sensation novel's preoccupation with crime, mystery and detection for what they saw as an attendant over-reliance on plot at the expense of character; Trollope even went so far as to claim that 'With Collins... it is all plot'.[26] The over-reliance on plot which some nineteenth-century reviewers saw as a major failing of the sensation novel has been seen by later critics as one of its more important achievements, signalling, as Ronald Thomas argues, 'the discovery that modern characters were tangled up in very complex social plots of class and pretense – mysteries that required a specialized expertise to expose' and to resolve.[27] In the sensation novel ordinary citizens become detectives and, in particular, lawyers and doctors engage in detection, using their special expertise and the proliferating array of nineteenth-century documentary records to establish a person's true identity or their culpability of a crime. The development of the exact science of detection that was to be practised by Conan Doyle's Sherlock Holmes assisted by Dr Watson is clearly anticipated in the sensation novel, not least in the way in which the central mystery of *The Moonstone* is resolved by the application of scientific expertise in an experimental re-enactment of the theft of the diamond.

The sensation novel also played an important part in the emergence of the female detective, from Marion Halcombe in *The Woman in White*, Barbara Hare in *East Lynne*, and Eleanor Vane in *Eleanor's Victory* in the 1860s through to Valeria Woodville/Macallan in *The Law and the Lady* in the mid-1870s. Alongside these women who turn detective in sensation novels, an early version of the New Woman began to emerge in professional female sleuths such Andrew Forrester's Mrs Gladden in *The Female Detective* (1864) and W. Stephens Hayward's Mrs Paschal in *Revelations of a Woman Detective* (1864). There was also a flowering of female detectives at the height of the New Woman debates in 1890s. Catherine Louisa Pirkis's professional female investigator Loveday Brooke made her appearance in a series of stories in *Ludgate Monthly* between February and July 1893, which were published (with one addition) as *The Experiences of Loveday Brooke, Lady Detective* in 1894. Other female detective novels of the 1890s included: George R. Sims's *Dorcas Dene, Detective* (1897), Fergus Hume's *Hagar of the Pawn Shop* (1899), L.T. Meades's *The Detections of Miss Cusack* (1899–1900), and Grant Allen's *Miss Cayley's Adventures* (1899). Pirkis's Loveday Brooke stories are a particularly interesting development of the sensation novel's focus on crime within the family and its preoccupation with household spies, as Brooke specializes in investigating robberies by entering households undercover in order to observe suspects at close quarters. This particular *modus operandi* is seen by Loveday's employer, Ebenezer Dyer, as particularly apt for female detectives. As Dyer notes in 'The Redhill Sisterhood', the 'idea seems to be gaining ground in many quarters that in cases of mere suspicion, women detectives are more satisfactory than men, for they are less likely to attract attention'.[28] Moreover, as he observes in 'The Black Bag Left on a Door-Step', a female detective is invaluable when the local police force 'want someone within the walls to hob-nob with the maids generally' and, in this particular case, to find out if a maid who is under suspicion has shared any confidences with the other servants.[29] As a professional detective a quarter of a century before the London Metropolitan police first employed female officers (in 1915),

Loveday is something of an outsider who transgresses social and gender boundaries in adapting resourcefully to the difficult hand that life has dealt her. Like many a sensation heroine, 'by a jerk of Fortune's wheel, Loveday had been thrown upon the world penniless and all but friendless', and, lacking 'marketable accomplishments... she had forthwith defied convention, and chosen for herself a career that had cut her off sharply from her former associates and her position in society'. However, unlike most sensation heroines, Loveday spends a number of years of patient drudgery in the 'lower walks of her profession' until 'an intricate criminal case threw her in the way of the experienced head of a flourishing detective agency' who, in turn, 'threw her in the way of better-class work'.[30]

Independence and the transgression of traditional gender roles (not least through the pursuit of professional work outside the domestic sphere) were, of course, characteristics of the New Women of the 1880s and 1890s, and of their fictional representation in New Woman novels. As I have noted elsewhere, despite initial appearances to the contrary, there are in fact a number of similarities between the popular sensation novels of the 1860s, with their 'bigamous or adulterous heroines and complicated plots of crime and intrigue, and the "modern women's books of the introspective type"... on the wrongs of women and the evils of men and marriage which appeared in the 1880s and 1890s'.[31] The sensation novel's reworking of female Gothic, melodrama and domestic realism anticipates the generic and stylistic hybridity of the New Woman fiction. Both kinds of novel expose and explore the contradictions of contemporary marriage and the domestic ideal and both were produced by and intervened in current debates about women's prescribed social, familial and gender roles. There were also remarkable similarities in the terms of the critical debates which the two kinds of fiction generated. In fact, in many ways the critical debate on the New Woman novel picked up some of the main threads of the sensation debate, focusing on transgressive, independent heroines, and repre-sentation of the female body and women's feelings.

By the end of the nineteenth century 'sensation' seems to take on a new guise, mutating into the political thriller. For example, the *Daily News*'s review of John K. Leys's *The Black*

Terror: A Romance of Russia describes it as being 'full of the usual secret society and secret police "business"' with 'good situations ingeniously treated' and 'cleverly and brightly told', and goes on to note that although 'Nihilism may be a danger to the country at large', it forms 'a very effective motive for that important institution the sensation novel'.[32] The sensation novel also provided an important model for one of the most significant early twentieth century novels about nihilism and terror, Joseph Conrad's *The Secret Agent* (1907). Edward Garnett was one of the first to link Conrad's novel to the sensation novel in his review in the *Nation* (28 September 1907), which commends the author for having 'brought clearly into our ken the subterranean world of that foreign London which, since the death of Count Fosco, has served in fiction only the crude purpose of our sensational writers'.[33] Perhaps surprisingly Conrad was an avid reader of Wood and Braddon. The latter was a special favourite, and *The Secret Agent* owes a great deal to *Lady Audley's Secret* as well as to *The Woman in White*. All three narratives share a common preoccupation with women's struggles with their domestic lot and the capacity for struggle and division within the secret theatre of home. Ellen Burton Harrington has suggested that Conrad's depiction of the supposedly emancipated woman Winnie Verloc is particularly indebted to the Victorian sensation novel, and that by ending his novel 'with the disintegration of the domestic sphere', Conrad 'makes an ironic commentary on gender roles... effectively referencing and re-envisioning the popular sensation novel and its themes of feminine frustration, the desire for liberation, and the dangers of degeneracy'.[34] Like the sensation novel, Harrington argues, *The Secret Agent* exposes the contradictions and problems of women's traditional roles whilst remaining ambivalent or troubled about the political and social implications of increasing women's autonomy.

THE NEO-SENSATION NOVEL

In his 1982 article 'What is "sensational" about the sensation novel?' Patrick Brantlinger suggested that the heirs of the nineteenth-century sensation novel are the popular genres of the twentieth-century – 'modern mystery, detective and suspense fiction and films'.[35] Since the late 1980s, however, the legacy of the sensation novel has also been evident in a growing number of self-consciously referential 'neo-Victorian' novels such as Sarah Waters's *Affinity* (1999) and *Fingersmith* (2002), James Wilson's *The Dark Clue* (2001), and Michael Faber's *The Crimson Petal and the White* (2002). Of these *The Dark Clue* and *Fingersmith* have the most direct link to the sensation novel, as the former is presented as a sequel to the narrative of *The Woman in White* and the latter borrows some of its dark atmosphere and plotting from Collins. *The Dark Clue* explores some of the possibilities of the *ménage à trois* in *The Woman in White* by leaving a pregnant Laura caring for her children at Limmeridge, while Marian and Hartright embark on an adventure in London when Hartright's role as J. M. W. Turner's biographer sets them on a quest to unravel the secrets of the painter's double life. Walter himself comes to lead a double life as his search takes him away from conventional middle-class society and his new role as a Victorian paterfamilias into the seamier side of London life. As they uncover Turner's buried life Walter and Marian are also shown as discovering something of their own buried lives and hidden desires. *Fingersmith* also deals with dark desires and the worlds of thieves and pornographers as well as prostitutes. The narration of this novel is shared between Sue, an orphan raised among thieves, who is involved in a plot to trick another orphan into marriage with the dashing criminal Richard Rivers, and Maud, the apparent victim of this plot. Virtually everyone in Waters's novel has at least one secret and the plot, which involves the substitution of one woman for another in a lunatic asylum, has more twists than Collins would have thought possible.

Beth Palmer has recently argued that the most significant and enduring legacy of sensation fiction is a 'self-consciousness about how the contemporary moment is constructed in and by print culture as it mediates the past',[36] as demonstrated by the neo-Victorian novels of Waters and Faber, which display a 'self-reflexive interest in the materiality of print culture',[37] and make knowing references to nineteenth-century sensation novels. Faber's massive, three-decker sized novel (of over 800 pages) includes the prostitute-heroine Sugar's fabrication of the death of the mad wife of her lover in order to save her from the lunatic asylum. The supposed death is reported in the form of a reprinted newspaper article, with the headline 'SECOND TRAGEDY BEFALLS RACKHAMS',[38] which recalls Helen Talboy's fake obituary in *Lady Audley's Secret*. Sarah Waters's *Affinity* deploys Collins's characteristic mode of dispersing narrative authority by constructing her narrative from the diaries of the two female protagonists, Margaret Prior, the neurasthenic, middle-class prison visitor and Selina Dawes, the prisoner (and spirit-medium) whom she visits, and whom she comes to desire. Both Faber and Waters also show how their characters' minds have been constructed by sensation novels. Faber does this in the form of knowing asides from his third person narrator, for example when Sugar suggests that her lover, Rackham, should employ a detective to search for his wife: '(She knows nothing about detectives beyond what she's read in *The Moonstone*, but she hopes the bumbling Seegraves outnumber the clever Cuffs)'.[39] Waters does it by dramatizing Margaret's attempt to explain the loss of her locket: 'perhaps I rose and seized the locket and placed it somewhere – like Franklin Blake in *The Moonstone*'.[40]

Referring to Peter Brooks's contention (in his Preface to *Reading For the Plot*) that the nineteenth century was the golden age of narrative, Kelly A. Marsh has noted a 're-emergence of sensation plotting'[41] in a much more diverse range of what she terms 'neo-sensation novels', which include: Graham Swift's *Waterland* (1983); Margaret Drabble's *The Radiant Way* (1987) and *A Natural Curiosity* (1989); A.S. Byatt's *Possession*; and *A Thousand Acres* (1991) and *The Gold Bug Variations* (1991) by the American novelists Jane Smiley and Richard Ford respectively. These 'neo-sensation novels', Marsh argues reveal 'a nostalgia for more than a vague notion of the "romance" of the Victorian tradition; it is a nostalgia for the nineteenth-century mind-set that could still believe that plot and closure bore some relationship to reality'.[42] These novels deploy the concept of sensation as 'an avenue to truth', and their return to a nineteenth-century form is the means of challenging the postmodern doctrine of unknowability and 'the notion of the unstable self which negates the possibility of free will and personal choice'.[43]

ADAPTATIONS OF THE SENSATION NOVEL FOR THE STAGE

> Once a tale becomes generally popular, a desire to see it as a dramatic form immediately spreads like an epidemic.[44]

From the outset the sensation novel had a complex relationship with the stage. The propensity of some sensation novelists for recycling other people's plots meant that they often drew on the stage repertoire. Sometimes they recycled their own dramatic plots. For example, the plot of Collins's novel, *Jezebel's Daughter* (1880,) was based on his play, *The Red Vial*, first staged at the Olympia Theatre in 1858. Moreover, as the epigraph at the head of this section indicates, popular fiction in general was a major source of material for playwrights. This, as well as the fact that the sensation novel boom at the beginning of the 1860s also coincided with a 'the development of a new genre of society melodrama',[45] meant that many sensation novels were adapted for the stage as soon as they had completed their original serial run. This was the certainly the case with *The Woman in White*, *Lady Audley's Secret*, and *Aurora Floyd*. Such adaptations were often unauthorized and by persons unknown to the author of the original novel, who usually received no fees or royalties from the dramatization of their work, unless they had established copyright by producing their own dramatization.[46] Many of these unauthorized adaptations, particularly those intended for working-class audiences, were very free appropriations of the original. Indeed this practice of 'tradaptation'[47] was one of the most important ways of disseminating sensation fiction to the lower classes. Stage adaptations toured widely in Britain and often also in Europe, Australia, Canada and the USA, thus augmenting the success of the sensation novel in Britain's colonies and former colonies.[48]

Lady Audley's Secret was dramatized almost immediately after the novel's publication, in at least twelve different versions. The dramatizations staged in London in 1862 included one by William E. Suter, which premièred at the Queen's Theatre on 21 February, a week before George Roberts's adaptation opened at the St James Theatre on 28 February. Colin H. Hazlewood's, version, which became one of the best known and most frequently performed adaptations of this novel, opened at the Victoria Theatre on 25 May. John Brougham's dramatic reworking of Braddon's novel, entitled *Where There's Life There's Hope*, was licensed on 30 June for production at the Strand.[49] The dramatizations by Suter, Hazlewood and Roberts all omit the character of Clara Talboys. As Collins did in his adaptations of his own sensation novels (see below), Hazlewood replaces the novel's emphasis on mystery (what is Lady Audley's secret?) with suspense (when will her secret be exposed?), by revealing the secret of the heroine's past in a soliloquy at the end of the first scene:

> I live now for ambition and interest, to mould the world and its votaries to my own end. Once I was fool enough to wed for love. Now I have married for wealth. What a change from the wife of George Talboys to the wife of Sir Michael Audley! My fool of a first husband thinks me dead. Oh excellent scheme, oh cunning device, how well you have served me.[50]

As Zoë Aldrich has noted, this soliloquy also marks Lady Audley as a new character type, which developed in the drama of the 1860s, the adventuress.[51] Unlike Braddon's adventuress, Hazlewood's is also unequivocally mad. At the end of the play the unmasked heroine dies of shock having uttered the following words, accompanied by the stage directions 'Laughs wildly':

> Mad, mad, that is the word. I feel it here, here! (*places her hand on her temples.*) Do not touch me ... let me claim your silence – your pity – and let the grave, the cold grave, close over Lady Audley and her secret . (*Falls – dies – Music – tableaux of sympathy – George Talboys kneels over her.*) CURTAIN.[52]

William Suter firmly located his adaptation in the genre of stage melodrama by adding a comic subplot, by presenting Lady Audley's pushing of George down the well as a premeditated murder attempt (she stabs him first), and by closing the play with Lady Audley's suicide (by poisoning). As in Hazlewood's play the curtain descends on a dramatic tableau of a group of shocked characters looking at the heroine's dead body. Braddon and her publisher disapproved of Suter's treatment of her novel and successfully sued for breach of copyright. However, this did not prevent Suter's play from further production, nor did it deter Suter from undertaking further adaptations of Braddon's novels. In March 1863 his stage adaptation of *Aurora Floyd, Aurora Floyd, or The Deed in the Wood,* was licensed to be performed at the Queen's Theatre. Like *Lady Audley's Secret, Aurora Floyd* proved very popular with adapters: a version by Charles Smith Cheltnam was licensed on 6 March 1863 for performance at the Princess's Theatre; Benjamin Webster's adaptation was licensed on 13 March for performance at the Adelphi, and in April Colin Hazlewood's *Aurora Floyd, or the first and second marriage* and J.B. Johnston's *Aurora Floyd,* a prologue and drama in two acts, were licensed for performance at the Britannia and Marylebone Theatres respectively.[53] In all, thirteen of Braddon's novels were adapted for the stage, including *The Black Band* (adapted by Robert Clark Allen), *Only a Clod* (adapted as *Caught in the Toils* by John Brougham), *The Cloven Foot* (by Frederick Mouillot) and *Henry Dunbar* (by Tom Taylor in 1865). *Lady Audley's Secret* remained part of the dramatic repertoire into the twentieth century, with several new adaptations. Two of them end with Lady Audley's suicide: in Brian Burton's *Lady Audley's Secret or The Lime Tree Walk,* first performed at the Little Theatre, Leicester in 1966, the heroine poisons herself in order to avoid incarceration in an asylum, and in Constance Cox's one-act melodrama published by Samuel French in 1976, she stabs herself following George's reappearance and Sir Michael's death. Sylvia Freedman's adaptation, first staged at the Lyric Theatre Hammersmith in 1991, updated Braddon's narrative for a late twentieth-century audience by allowing Lady Audley to escape from the asylum and adopt a new identity. There has also been at least one musical version of *Lady Audley's Secret,* with music by George Goehring, book by Douglas Seale and lyrics by John Kunz (1972). The short-running production at the Eastside Playhouse Theatre, New York, was described as 'mannered, macabre and mercilessly mirthful musical melodrama'.[54]

Ellen Wood's *East Lynne* was first adapted for the stage by J. W. Archer under the title of *Marriage Bells: or the Cottage on the Cliff.* It was produced at the Effingham Theatre at Whitechapel in the East End of London in November 1864. Like Wood's novel, Archer's adaptation is a cautionary tale of seduction and betrayal focusing on the downfall of Emily, the aristocratic wife of Mordaunt, a well-to-do solicitor, as a result of her seduction by the dissolute aristocrat, Captain Alfred, who persuades her that her husband is in love with their neighbour, Barbara. However, as Andrew Maunder has demonstrated, Archer's play reworks Wood's novel for a working-class audience by emphasizing working-class poverty and the gap between the rich and poor.[55] Archer's adaptation omits the train crash and the disfiguring injuries; in this adaptation the adulterous heroine, abandoned by her lover, returns to London with her illegitimate child and tramps the streets in search of work. Helpless and unfriended like the typical heroine of working-class melodrama,[56] Emily is rescued from the brink of suicide by working-class Fanny Hillford who draws her into 'a new web of [working-class] affiliation'.[57] Driven by maternal longing, the disguised Emily returns to the Mordaunt household to work as governess to her own children, but she is quickly discovered and banished from her children's presence to die of a wasting illness and a broken heart.

Just over a year after the first performance of Effingham's adaptation of Wood's novel, on 5 February 1866, the New Surrey Theatre staged what it billed as the première of *East Lynne*, dramatized by John Oxenford and starring the American actress, Avonia Jones as Lady Isabel. Oxenford's adaptation, which emphasized the importance for middle-class women of adhering to their marital and maternal duties, was an immediate critical and popular success and transferred to the West End theatre, the Lyceum, a year later. In various different adaptations *East Lynne* became a useful standby and guaranteed money-earner for theatre managers and performers for the rest of the century. The most successful of the fifteen or so nineteenth-century stage adaptations was probably T.A. Palmer's, first performed in Nottingham on 19 November 1874 with Madge Robertson as Lady Isabel. Although she lamented the lack of direct personal financial gain from these productions, Wood took comfort in the belief that their popularity brought her additional readers and book sales. As she observed to her publisher George Bentley in 1875:

> I cannot help thinking that a portion of 'East Lynne's' success is owing to it being so much represented on stage. Go where I will, I mean into country places, I am sure to see the walls placarded with 'East Lynne'. People see the play and next day they buy the book.[58]

Stage productions of *East Lynne* continued – with reduced frequency – into and through the twentieth century in the UK, Australia and the USA. For example it was part of the repertory of the Sydney Music Hall which operated between 1961 and 1980 (as was *Lady Audley's Secret*). The most recent adaptation was commissioned from Lisa Evans by the Birmingham Repertory Theatre in 1992. Evans's version has also been produced in Denmark, at the Redgrave Theatre in Farnham, the Greenwich Theatre and, in July 2005, at London's New Vic. In the 1970s *East Lynne* was also adapted as a musical in two acts by the American writers Robert Neil Porter and Jack Perry (published by Pioneer Drama Service, Denver Colorado, 1977).

The dramatization of Collins's sensation novels for the nineteenth-century stage is particularly interesting because Collins, an experienced and successful playwright and enthusiastic actor, undertook the task himself. Collins dramatizations of his own novels were, as Richard Pearson has noted, 'rereadings or even counter-readings' of them.[59] The first stage adaptation of *The Woman in White* was a pirated three-act drama by J. Reddington Ware, performed at the Surrey Theatre in Lambeth in November 1860, a few months after the completion of the novel's serial run in August and coinciding with its publication in three volumes. Further adaptations followed rapidly: W. Sidney's version was staged at the Theatre Royal, Norwich in January 1861, an unattributed adaptation opened at London's Sadler's Wells Theatre in August 1861, and, in September 1862, The Theatre Royal, Cambridge staged Josephine Fiddes's adaptation, with the young Henry Irving as Hartright. Stage adaptations of *The Woman in White* were not confined to Britain. In Australia a version by the English actor-dramatist George Fawcett Rowe was staged at the Princess's Theatre in Melbourne in March 1862, and in Europe adaptations were staged in Berlin (December 1866), Rotterdam, the Hague and Delft (1870).[60]

In 1871, just over ten years after *The Woman in White* began its serial publication, Collins's own dramatization of his novel was first performed at the Olympic Theatre, where it enjoyed a nineteen-week run. A critical as well as popular success, Collins's stage version of *The Woman in White* was very different from his novel. In particular it played down the novel's sensationalism. The dramatic scene in which Hartright first meets Anne Catherick on the road to Hampstead is dropped, and Sir Percival's death (in this version a death by drowning as he seeks to escape to France in a fishing boat) occurs off stage. Collins also cut down the novel's complex cast of characters, compressed the narrative, and did not attempt to preserve its mysteries. Thus, for example, in a scene not included in the novel, his stage version makes clear from the outset the precise nature of the relationship between Anne and Laura. The result is a play which, far from seeking to emulate the spectacular theatre and the sensation drama of the 1860s, anticipated 'the more psychological dramas of the final quarter of the nineteenth century'.[61]

Twentieth-century stage adaptations of *The Woman in White* include Tim Kelly's irreverently melodramatic version entitled *Egad, The Woman in White* (1975), and, perhaps the most surprising recent example of the after-life of the sensation novel, Andrew Lloyd Webber's musical *The Woman in White*, which opened at the Palace Theatre in London in 2004, just as Lloyd Webber's *Les Misérables* ended its nineteen-year run. With lyrics by David Zippel (whose previous work includes *City of Angels*, a spoof on 1940s detective movies), a book by Charlotte Jones (who had earlier updated *Hamlet* in her play *Humble Boy*), and directed by Trevor Nunn, this loose adaptation of Collins's novel follows recent television adaptations (see below) by putting Marian at the centre. However, it also transforms her into a lovesick woman pining for Walter's affection, one whose constant refrain is 'I close my eyes and still I see his face'. This Lloyd Webber extravaganza evokes the sensation drama's use of modern technology with its use of shifting video projections for the novel's multiple settings and, at one point, to simulate a railway train rushing noisily out of tunnel as if about to crash into the stalls. The fact that the whole production 'clearly offers a branded "Lloyd Webber" experience, complete with souvenir tapestry kits and pill-boxes', as Rachel Malik puts it, indicates the degree to which it is 'shaped by the contexts and forms of... sensation fiction and the mid-Victorian practices of writing and publishing popular fiction'.[62]

Collins published his four-act dramatization of *No Name* in 1870, but like William Bayle Bernard's five-act adaption (1863) it was not performed in Britain. However, an adaptation by the actor Wybert Reeve was staged in New York in 1871, and subsequently in Australia. Collins published a limited edition of a stage version of *Armadale* in 1866 in order to protect his copyright. He later collaborated with his friend François Regnier on an adaptation intended for a French performance, but instead first staged the play, *Miss Gwilt*, at the Alexandra Theatre in Liverpool in December 1875. In *Miss Gwilt* Doctor Downward was made the villain of the piece and Lydia became a much more sympathetic character than she had been in the novel. The play subsequently transferred to London's Globe Theatre in April 1876 where its twelve-week run suggests that it was a popular success. However, when one compares this with the twenty-three week run of *Man and Wife* at the Prince of Wales Theatre (from February 1873), and *The New Magdalen's* nineteen-week run at the Olympic (from May 1873), it would appear that by 1875 Collins's dramatic star was beginning to wane.

Collins's dramatization of *The Moonstone* had what was, for Collins, a rather modest nine-week run after it opened at the Royal Olympic Theatre in London in September 1877. The somewhat disappointing reception of this play led Collins to abandon plans for an American production, but did not cause him to revise his own view of its merits; as he wrote to the American playwright and director Augustin Daly on 10 December 1877, '[i]n spite of the indifference of the public reception here, I think it myself one of the best things of the kind that I have written'.[63] What kind of thing was this drama in four acts? Like many stage adaptations of novels it had fewer characters and settings than the original. Collins's dramatization had no Rosanna Spearman, Limping Lucy, Ezra Jennings, Indians or Murthwaite, and its action was condensed to a twenty-four hour period in a single setting, the hallway of Rachel Verinder's country house. The restriction of setting makes the focus of the play more singularly domestic than the novel, and it also significantly reduces the concern with Empire. The play also makes less of the original imperial theft of the diamond. When it is recovered from its most recent thief it is sold by Rachel who invests the proceeds in improving the conditions of the poor in her neighbourhood. The play relies for its effects not so much on mystery and sensation as on suspense.

There is no mystery about the theft of the diamond – the audience sees Franklin take it as he sleepwalks. Nor is there any real mystery about the sleepwalking. Franklin has not been secretly drugged with laudanum, but, having eaten and drunk too well, sleepwalks and acts out his anxieties about the diamond's safety. Collins's play also departs from the sensation novel's tendency to punish its villains without recourse to law. In the play Godfrey Ablewhite is not murdered by the diamond's Indian guardians, but leaves the stage having been unmasked by Cuff, who assures his audience that a policeman awaits him outside.

SENSATION NOVELS IN SOUND AND ON SCREEN

As well as providing a rich resource for the nineteenth century theatre repertoire, which continued into the twentieth and twenty-first centuries, the sensation novels of Braddon, Collins and Wood – and the various dramatic adaptations of them – were also a fruitful source for new silent moving pictures which began to supplement – and then replace – the melodramatic theatre in the early twentieth century. Sensation novels soon established themselves as part of the silent cinema repertoire, and their plots were later drawn on by the writers and producers of films with sound. In the second half of the twentieth century sensation novels were also adapted for the modern form of cultural production and reception that most closely resembles the practice of family reading – the radio or television serial. Adaptations of Collins's novels were first introduced in 'genre' slots, such as ABC's 'The Hour of Mystery' in the UK and NBC's the 'Dow Hour of Great Mysteries' in the USA. In the latter half of the twentieth century sensation novels entered the 'classic serial' repertory on television and radio.

Of all of the sensationalists, it is Collins whose work has been most frequently translated to the screen and radio. Collins's novels provided the plot material for at least twelve silent films between 1909 and 1929: one based on *The Dead Secret* (USA, directed by Stanner E.V. Taylor, 1913), three on *The Woman in White* (1912, 1913 and 1929), one on *Armadale* (USA, directed by Richard Garrick, 1916), three on *The Moonstone* (1909, 1911 and

1915) and four on *The New Magdalen* (1910, 1912, 1913 and 1914).

The Woman in White is the novel which has been most frequently translated into other media. Its basic plot – simplified as a story of the persecution and imprisonment of vulnerable women by sinister aristocrats and their rescue by a modest, noble young hero – lent itself particularly well to the melodramatic treatment of the silent movie. For example the 1912 production by the Tannhauser Film Corporation in the USA omits the characters of Fosco and Marian Halcombe and makes the story into the drama of two women and two men: Anne Catherick, Laura Fairlie, Walter Hartright and Sir Percival Glyde. This version relies heavily on newly invented dramatic scenes, such as the one in which Anne confronts Sir Percival with the words 'I am not mad, and you are not Sir Percival', and then dies of shock at the ferocity of his response, or the one in which, having noted Anne's close physical resemblance to Laura, Glyde poisons his wife and leaves her prone body at the gates of the lunatic asylum, where she is discovered and assumed to be the escaped lunatic Anne. In this film version Walter is not required to be a detective. Instead, Glyde's secret is uncovered by a servant who comes across the book in which Anne has scrawled – in her own blood – a message about where the proof of Glyde's true identity may be found. Glyde makes a dying confession before perishing in the church which he has set ablaze by accidentally upsetting a lamp. The second American silent movie adaptation (by Gem), also omits Marian, but gives a prominent place to Fosco, who, in this version, is the heroine's guardian.

The first British film adaptation of *The Woman in White*, a silent movie directed by Herbert Wilcox, released in 1929, adhered more closely to Collins's novel than had the earlier American versions. It is also more successful in conveying the air of strangeness and mystery of the original story. Its most significant innovation was the treatment of Fosco's death as a suicide. Another British production, *Crimes at the Dark House*, a talkie, directed by George King and released in 1940, is rather loosely based on Collins's novel. It is mainly a vehicle for Tod Slaughter, one of the great barnstormers of the melodramatic theatre, who appears in the role of an evil count who gets an escapee from an asylum to masquerade as his murdered wife.

137

Warner Brothers's 1947 release, directed by Peter Godfrey and starring Sydney Greenstreet as Fosco, takes some liberties with Collins's novel and, perhaps, takes up some of its ambiguities about gender roles and the fluidity and multiplicity of relationships, by providing an ending in which Laura, having borne Glyde's child, finds fulfilment in motherhood, and Walter proclaims his love for Marian.

The Moonstone also proved popular with early twentieth-century filmmakers. The first silent movie adaptation, produced in the USA by Selig Polyscope in 1909, made much of Franklin's hypnotic trance, while a French version by Pathé in 1911 focused on the curse which is visited on those who interfere with the diamond. A second American silent version, directed by Frank Hall Crane in 1915, stuck fairly closely to Collins's original. On the other hand, the first sound version, directed by Reginald Barker in 1934 for the American studio Monogram, set Collins's narrative in the 1930s and renamed some of the characters. In this version Franklin and his Hindu servant arrive on a stormy night at the home of the doctor, Sir John Verinder, in order that Franklin may deliver a diamond – which, as in Collins's novel was stolen from an Indian temple in 1799 – to his fiancée Anne Verinder. The diamond is stolen from its hiding place under Anne's pillow as she sleeps, and Inspector Cuff is called in to question the inmates of the house. These include Betteredge, here transformed into a female housekeeper and Godfrey Ablewhite, a dealer in rare books. A delirious Sir John Verinder subsequently reveals that he had drugged Franklin's bedtime milk on the night of the theft and Cuff arranges for Franklin to be given another drugged nightcap – without his co-operation or prior knowledge (unlike the novel).

The most recent cinema adaptation of a sensation novel by Collins is Radha Bharadwaj's film of *Basil*, starring Christian Slater and first shown on the American Movie Classics Channel in November 1998. Written, directed and produced by Bharadwaj, *Basil* has a fairly lengthy opening section on the hero's childhood and early youth that expands considerably on Collins's novel, giving its own gloss on Basil's family situation. The opening section also stages the first meeting between Basil and Mannion, in which the latter saves the hero from drowning. It is also Mannion, rather than a chance meeting on an omnibus, who is the means of introducing Basil to his future wife 'Julia' (as Margaret Sherwin is renamed). Bharadwaj develops the novel's preoccupation with money, class and cross-class relations, by presenting Julia as an avaricious woman who responds contemptuously to Basil's overtures, marries him for his wealth and social status and conducts a long secret affair with Mannion. In an updating of the revenge plot, Mannion's behaviour towards Basil is explained in terms of his desire to avenge his sister who has died from a botched abortion following her seduction and betrayal by Basil's brother.

Serialized adaptations of Collins's fiction have featured prominently on radio and television. A far from exhaustive list of the radio adaptation of Collins's sensation novels includes: a two-part dramatization of *Basil* by Robin Brooks for BBC Radio 4 in 2006; a four-part dramatization of *The Woman in White* by Martyn Wade (Radio 4, 2001), and a reading in eight episodes (Radio 4, 2004); a six-part adaptation of *No Name* (Radio 4, 1973), and a two-part dramatization by John Fletcher in 1989, as well as an earlier BBC radio adaptation in 1962; a 1948 radio version of *Armadale* and Robin Brooks's three-part dramatization of this novel for Radio 4 in 2009; a 1945 adaptation of *The Moonstone* for the syndicated American radio series 'The Weird Circle', and a six-episode dramatization for Radio 4 in 1979.

The Woman in White was first dramatized for British television in 1957 as a short anthology piece in ABC Television's 'Hour of Mystery', and an American adaptation in 1960 was first aired as part of 'The Dow Hour of Great Mysteries'. This novel was first given the full BBC Sunday Classic treatment in a six-part adaptation by Michael Voysey in 1966, with the same actress (Jennifer Hilary) playing the parts of Laura and Anne. The first version for colour television, adapted by Ray Jenkins, appeared on BBC2 in five, fifty-five minute episodes in 1982 (shown in the USA in 1985). This production's independent and spirited representation of Laura (played by Jenny Seagrove), and Marian (Diana Quick) perhaps owe something to the women's movement of the 1970s. In 1997 a two-part dramatization of *The Woman in White* (a BBC, Carlton and WGBH Boston co-production) filled a 'Christmas Special' slot, thus returning Collins to one of his original contexts as the producer (with Dickens) of special Christmas Numbers of *Household Words*, as well as placing the novel in the twenty-first century heritage movie category. David Pirie's adaptation, directed by Tim Fywell, followed the modern tendency to focus on Marian. She is the first character both seen and heard by the audience, and her voice-overs propel the narrative, replacing Walter as its editor and shaper. This updated Marian is more active and more sexually knowing than Collins's original, as is Walter, who learns how to be a man by journeying into darkest London rather than South American jungles. The violence against women and their sexual exploitation, which is implicit in the social structure about which Collins writes is, in this adaptation (in common with most late-twentieth century adaptations of Collins's sensation novels), made explicit: Laura is represented as the victim of physical domestic violence and Anne as the victim of child sex abuse. In an updating of the novel's sensationalism Anne is a tormented rather than distracted character, and her final act of desperation is to commit suicide by jumping from a tower.

Thus far there have been three BBC TV dramatizations of *The Moonstone* – a seven-part version shot in black and white in 1959, a five-part version in 1973, and a two-part Christmas special (the first of Collins's novels to receive this treatment) in 1996, with a screenplay by Kevin Elyot, the author of a stage adaptation of *The Moonstone*, first performed in 1990. Elyot's screenplay for the 1996 BBC adaptation, relied heavily on Betteredge (played by Peter Vaughan), who reads out letters which explain the plot and picks up and communicates essential plot information. Elyot's Cuff, as played by Antony Sher, emphasizes and augments the quirks of Collins's detective and reminds the modern television audience just how much their favourite TV detectives owe to this nineteenth-century original. This adaptation emphasizes and updates Collins's preoccupation with class, empire, and unusual mental states. The opening and closing titles roll over atmospheric shots of the Shivering Sands, later the setting of a powerful scene in which the love-sick servant Rosanna commits suicide. The opening shots of the Shivering Sands are followed by a scene dramatizing the original violent theft of the Indian diamond, immediately revealed as a dream which Franklin has whilst sleeping beside his wife. The film also closes with a dreamlike scene showing the purification of the

Brahmins, which cuts to a repeat of the shot of Franklin and Rachel sleeping in their marital bed. These juxtaposed scenes suggest the oriental otherness of the Indians and invoke Empire as a persistent and troubling component of the British psyche, as well as a material fact underpinning the comfortable lives of Franklin and Rachel. The closing title shot of the Shivering Sands reminds the viewer of the troubled working-class girl Rosanna.

Lady Audley's Secret found its way into two American silent films, one directed by Otis Turner in 1912, and another, *The Secrets of Society*, directed by Marshall Farnum in 1915. The first British silent version, directed by Jack Denton for the Ideal Company in 1920, begins by dramatizing the novel's 'back story' in scenes showing Lady Audley's meeting with and marriage to George and then her progress from the drab, shabby gentility of her home to the splendour of Audley Court. In a further development of the back story, Denton enhances George's role, and makes him seem more of a victim, by intercutting Helen/ Lucy's story with shots of George maintaining a lonely watch by his campfire in Australia. Denton also updates Braddon's heroine, transforming her from girl of the period to a feisty, cigarette-smoking, bobbed-haired new woman. However, Denton follows earlier stage adapters of the novel by making Lady Audley ultimately a figure of pathos who dies by her own hand: the film's penultimate scene shows Lady Audley swallowing a handful of pills after being tormented by the appearance of what she takes to be George's ghost, and the final scene shows her maid mourning the mistress whose dead body she has just discovered.

Aurora Floyd has proved less popular with film makers than *Lady Audley's Secret*, but there were two silent film versions produced in the USA in 1912 (directed by Theodore Marston) and 1915 (directed by Travers Vale). Braddon's fiction had to await its largely feminist-inspired rediscovery before it was translated to television and radio. *Lady Audley's Secret* was dramatized in two parts by Bryony Lavery for BBC Radio 4 in 1999, and a new version, directed by Julie Beckett and Fiona Kelcher, was broadcast as the Radio 4 Woman's Hour serial in 2009. Donald Hounam's adaptation for an ITV, Carlton Television and Warner Sisters co-production, directed by Betsan

Morris Evans was first broadcast on ITV and US public broadcasting in 2000. Hounam displeased many Braddon aficionados by taking as many liberties with the novel as had its nineteenth-century adapters. Like most of them he omitted Clara Talboys and he changed Braddon's ending. In Hounam's adaptation a perfectly sane Lady Audley escapes from the asylum assisted by her stepdaughter Alicia, who has an improbably sympathetic relationship with the dark-haired (rather than Braddon's blonde) beauty who bewitched both her father and her cousin. Where Braddon's novel suggests Robert's fascination with his aunt by marriage, Hounam emphasizes his infatuation with this *femme fatale*, who he last sees at a railway station accompanied by a man – perhaps her third husband.[64]

Early film versions of *East Lynne* were adaptations of the stage versions rather than the novel. Silent movie versions in 1916 and 1925 starred Theda Bara and Alma Rubens in the heroine's role, and a lavish American-produced early talkie (1931), starring Ann Harding and Clive Brook, received an Oscar nomination for Best Picture. Another 1931 release was the popular British farce *East Lynne on the Western Front*, in which soldiers attempt to put on a production of the play. In 1919 Paramount released the comedy *East Lynne with variations* for which Mack Sennett wrote the screenplay. Wood entered the BBC cannon rather earlier than Braddon and thus far there have been two BBC television adaptations of *East Lynne* – in 1976 (starring Polly James) and 1982 (directed by David Green). Michael Bakewell's radio dramatization of Wood's novel was first broadcast on BBC Radio 4 in seven one-hour episodes in 1987 to coincide with the centenary of Wood's death.

These numerous adaptations and mediations of sensation novels in a range of media, and in quite different historical and cultural contexts from those in which they were originally produced and read, are not only evidence of the continuing appeal of sensation, but also suggest something of the ambiguity of sensation novels and (to paraphrase a recent critic) their openness to alternative readings, especially in relation to issues of gender and class.[65]

Notes

CHAPTER 1. THE SENSATION PHENOMENON

1. 'Women's Novels', *The Broadway*, n.s., 1(1868), 504–9, reprinted in Andrew Maunder (ed.), *Varieties of Women's Sensation Fiction, 1855–1890* (London: Pickering and Chatto, 2004), vol.1, 220.
2. 'Sensation Novels', *Quarterly Review*, 133 (1863), 512.
3. 'What is Sensational About the Sensation Novel?, *Nineteenth Century Fiction*, 37 (1982), 1.
4. Ibid, 4.
5. P.D. Edwards, *Some Mid-Victorian Thrillers: The Sensation Novel, Its Friends and Its Foes* (St Lucia: University of Queensland Press, 1971), 4.
6. Thomas Richards, *The Commodity Culture of Victorian England: Advertising and Spectacle, 1851–1914* (Stanford: Stanford University Press, 1990), 55.
7. See Rebecca Gill, 'The Imperial Anxieties of a Nineteenth-Century Bigamy Case', *History Workshop Journal*, 57 (2004), 58–78.
8. Jenny Bourne Taylor, *In the Secret Theatre of Home: Wilkie Collins, Sensation Narrative and Nineteenth-Century Psychology* (London: Routledge, 1988).
9. This case is the subject of Kate Summerscale's fascinating account, *The Suspicions of Mr Whicher, or, The Murder at Road Hill House* (London: Bloomsbury, 2008).
10. See Thomas Boyle, *Black Swine in the Sewers of Hampstead: Beneath the Surface of Victorian Sensationalism* (London: Hodder and Stoughton, 1989).
11. 'The Queen's English', *Edinburgh Review*, 120 (1864), 53.
12. Cit. K.Tillotson, Introduction to *The Woman in White* (Boston: Houghton Mifflin, 1969), xiii.
13. Edwards, op. cit., 4.
14. Margaret Oliphant, 'Novels', *Blackwood's*, 94 (1867), 29.
15. Andrew Maunder, 'Mapping the Victorian Sensation Novel', *Literature Compass*, 2 (2005), 19.

16. Henry Longueville Mansel, 'Sensation Novels', *Quarterly Review*, 113 (1863), 491.
17. Cit., Norman Page (ed.), *Wilkie Collins, The Critical Heritage* (London: Routledge and Kegan Paul, 1974), 169.
18. Margaret Oliphant, 'Sensation Novels', *Blackwood's*, 91 (1862), 565.
19. 'Belles Lettres', *Westminster Review*, 20 (1866), 269.
20. Mansel, op. cit., 482–3.
21. Alison Winter, *Mesmerized: Powers of Mind in Victorian Britain* (Chicago: Chicago University Press, 1998), 224.
22. Mansel, op. cit., 487.
23. 'Our Female Sensation Novelists', *Christian Remembrancer*, 46 (1864), 210.
24. Kate Flint, *The Woman Reader, 1837–1914* (Oxford: Oxford University Press, 1993), 274.
25. 'Madness in Novels', *Spectator*, 3 Feb 1866, 135–6.
26. Henry James, 'Miss Braddon', *The Nation*, 9 November 1865, 594.
27. Ibid.
28. E.S. Dallas, *The Gay Science* (London: Chapman and Hall, 1866), vol.2, 296.
29. 'Novels', *Blackwood's*, 102 (1867), 209.
30. *Broadway* (1866), in Maunder, *Varieties of Women's Sensation Fiction*, vol.1, 220.
31. Tzvetan Todorov, *Mikhail Bakhtin: The Dialogical Principle*, trans. W. Godzick (Manchester: Manchester University Press, 1984), 80.
32. Frederick Jameson, *The Political Unconscious: Narrative as a Socially Symbolic Act* (London: Methuen, 1981), 141.
33. Mansel, op. cit., 486.
34. Oliphant, *Blackwood's*, 91 (1862), 569.
35. Mansel, op. cit., 484.
36. Ibid, 485.
37. Ibid, 483.
38. See Beth Kalikoff, *Murder and Moral Decay in Victorian Popular Literature* (Ann Arbor: University of Michigan Press, 1986); Winifred Hughes, *The Maniac in the Cellar: The Sensation Novel of the 1860s* (Princeton, NJ: Princeton University Press, 1980); Jennifer Carnell, *The Literary Lives of M.E. Braddon* (Hastings: The Sensation Press, 2000); Dallas Liddle, 'Anatomy of a "Nine Day's Wonder": Sensational Journalism in the Decade of the Sensation Novel', in Andrew Maunder and Grace Moore (eds.), *Victorian Crime, Madness and Sensation* (Aldershot: Ashgate, 2004).
39. W. Fraser Rae, 'Sensation Novelists: Miss Braddon', *North British Review*, 43 (1865), 204.
40. Lyn Pykett, *The Improper Feminine: The Women's Sensation Novel and the New Woman Writing* (London: Routledge, 1992).

41. Kalikoff, op.cit., 97.
42. Dallas Liddle, op. cit., 97.
43. See Peter Brooks, *The Melodramatic Imagination* (New Haven: Yale University Press, 1976).
44. Elaine Hadley, *Melodramatic Tactics: Theatricalized Dissent in the English Marketplace, 1800–1885* (Stanford: Stanford University Press, 1995), 3.
45. Ibid.
46. Martha Vicinus, '"Helpless and Unfriended": Nineteenth-Century Domestic Melodrama', *New Literary History*, 13 (1981), 128.
47. Brooks, op. cit., 11–12.
48. Mansel, op. cit., 485.
49. See Jennifer Phegley, 'Teaching Genre: The Sensation Novel' in Andrew Maunder and Jennifer Phegley (eds.), *Teaching Nineteenth-Century Fiction* (Palgrave Macmillan, 2010), 91–108.
50. Tamar Heller 'Recent Work on Victorian Gothic and Sensation Fiction', *Victorian Literature and Culture*, 24 (1996), 349.
51. Ibid.
52. Jenny Bourne Taylor, op. cit., 3.
53. Nicholas Daly, *Literature, Technology and Modernity, 1860–2000* (Cambridge: Cambridge University Press, 2004), 3.
54. Ibid, 37.
55. Ibid, 49.
56. Andrew Maunder, 'Mapping the Victorian Sensation Novel', 19.
57. See Andrew Maunder (ed.), *Varieties of Women's Sensation Fiction, 1855–1890* (London: Pickering and Chatto, 2004), 6 vols. In vol.1 Maunder provides a lengthy bibliography of sensation novels.
58. Maunder, 'Mapping the Victorian Sensation Novel', 20.
59. See, for example: Jennifer Phegley, *Educating the Proper Woman Reader: Victorian Literary Family Magazines and the Cultural Health of the Nation* (Ohio: Ohio State University Press, 2004); Jennifer Carnell and Graham Law, '"Our Author": Braddon in the Provincial Weeklies', in Marlene Tromp, Pamela Gilbert and Aeron Haynie (eds.) *Beyond Sensation: Mary Elizabeth Braddon in Context* (Albany: SUNY Press, 2000), 127–164; Graham Law, *Serializing Fiction in the Victorian Press* (Basingstoke: Palgrave Macmillan, 2000); Graham Law and Andrew Maunder, *Wilkie Collins: A Literary Life* (Basingstoke: Palgrave Macmillan, 2008).
60. Letter from Mary Elizabeth Braddon, cit., Robert Lee Wolff, *Sensational Victorian: The Life and Fiction of Mary Elizabeth Braddon* (New York: Garland, 1979), 126.
61. Andrew King, 'Sympathy as Subversion? Reading *Lady Audley's Secret* in the Kitchen', *Journal of Victorian Culture*, 7 (2002), 60–85.
62. Kate Flint, 'The Woman Reader and the Opiate of Fiction', in

Jeremy Hawthorn (ed.), *The Nineteenth-Century British Novel* (London: Arnold, 1988), 47–61.

63. See Pamela Gilbert, *Disease, Desire and the Body in Victorian Women's Popular Novels* (Cambridge: Cambridge University Press, 2005), and Susan Bernstein, 'Dirty Reading: Sensation Fiction, Women and Primitivism'. *Criticism* 36 (1994), 213–41.
64. Phegley, op. cit., 2.
65. Phegley, op. cit., 22.
66. Raymond Williams, *The Long Revolution* (Harmondsworth: Penguin 1965), 67.

CHAPTER 2. WILKIE COLLINS

1. Winifred Hughes, *The Maniac in the Cellar: The Sensation Novel of the 1860s* (Princeton, NJ: Princeton University Press, 1980), 138.
2. T. S. Eliot, 'Wilkie Collins and Dickens', *Times Literary Supplement*, 4 August 1927, 525–26; reprinted in *Selected Essays: 1917–1932* (London: Faber, 1932).
3. Jenny Bourne Taylor (ed.), *The Cambridge Companion to Wilkie Collins* (Cambridge: Cambridge University Press, 2006), 1.
4. 'Esmond and Basil', *Bentley's Miscellany* 32 (Dec, 1852), 576.
5. Geraldine Jewsbury, *Athenaeum*, 24 June 1854, 775; reprinted in Norman Page (ed.), *Wilkie Collins, The Critical Heritage* (London: Routledge and Kegan Paul, 1974), 56.
6. Jenny Bourne Taylor, *In the Secret Theatre of Home: Wilkie Collins, Sensation Narrative and Nineteenth-Century Psychology* (London: Routledge, 1988), 72.
7. Gordon Haight, *George Eliot: A Biography* (Oxford: Oxford University Press, 1968), 144.
8. Unsigned Review, *The Leader*, 24 June 1854, 519; reprinted in Page, op.cit., 57.
9. See Taylor, *In the Secret Theatre of Home* and Elaine Showalter, *The Female Malady: Women, Madness and English Culture* (London: Virago, 1987).
10. See William M. Clarke, *The Secret Life of Wilkie Collins* (London: Allison & Busby, 1988).
11. Wilkie Collins, *My Miscellanies* (London: Sampson Low, 1863), vol. 1, 84.
12. H. F. Chorley, *Athenaeum*, 22 June 1866, 732; reprinted in Page, op. cit., 146.
13. Hughes, op.cit., 159.
14. Margaret Oliphant, 'Novels' *Blackwood's*, 94 (1863), 168–83; reprinted in Page, op. cit., 143.

15. Walter Benjamin, *Charles Baudelaire: A Lyric Poet in the Era of High Capitalism* (London: Verso, 1973), 40.

16. Eve Kosofsky Sedgwick, *Between Men: English Literature and Male Homosocial Desire* (New York: Columbia University Press, 1985).

17. Lillian Nayder, *Wilkie Collins*, (New York: Twayne, 1997), 107.

18. See Frederick Jameson, *The Political Unconscious: Narrative as a Socially Symbolic Act* (London: Methuen, 1981).

19. Patrick Brantlinger, 'What is Sensational About the Sensation Novel?', *Nineteenth Century Fiction*, 37 (1982), 14.

20. Raymond Williams, *The English Novel From Dickens to Lawrence* (London: Hogarth Press, 1985), 16.

21. See, for example, A.C. Swinburne's comment in his retrospect on Collins's career which appeared in the *Fortnightly Review* just over a month after the novelist's death: 'there are many who think that Wilkie Collins would have a likelier chance of a longer life in the memories of future readers if he had left nothing behind him but his masterpiece *The Moonstone* and one or two other stories'; reprinted in Page, op. cit., 259.

22. Unsigned Review of *Jezebel's Daughter*, *Spectator*, 15 May 1880, 627; reprinted in Page, op. cit., 208.

23. Andrew Maunder and Graham Law, *Wilkie Collins: A Literary Life* (Basingstoke: Palgrave Macmillan, 2008), 172.

CHAPTER 3. THE WOMEN'S SENSATION NOVEL

1. 'Women's Novels', *The Broadway*, n.s. 1 (1868), 504; reprinted in Maunder, *Varieties of Women's Sensation Fiction, 1855–1890* (London: Pickering and Chatto, 2004), 220–1.

2. E.S. Dallas, 'Lady Audley's Secret', *The Times*, 18 November 1862, 8.

3. 'Novels Past and Present', *Saturday Review*, 14 April 1866, 438.

4. Frances Paget, Afterword to *Lucretia: or the Heroine of the Nineteenth Century* (London: J. Masters, 1868); reprinted in Maunder op. cit., 215.

5. M. Oliphant, 'Novels', *Blackwood's*, 102 (1867), 275.

6. See Lyn Pykett, *The Improper Feminine: The Women's Sensation Novel and the New Woman Writing* (London: Routledge, 1992); Nancy Armstrong, *Desire and Domestic Fiction* (New York: Oxford University Press, 1987).

7. Alfred Austin, 'The Poetry of the Period: Mr Swinburne', *Temple Bar*, 26 (1869), 457–74.

8. Cit., R.L. Wolff, *Sensational Victorian: The Life and Fiction of Mary Elizabeth Braddon* (New York: Garland, 1979), 193.

9. Jane Tompkins, *Sensational Designs: The Cultural Work of American*

Fiction, 1790–1816 (Oxford: Oxford University Press, 1985), 123.

10. Tania Modleski, *Loving With a Vengeance: Mass-Produced Fantasies for Women* (London: Methuen, 1984), 25.

11. Ibid, 20.

12. Janice Radway, *Reading the Romance: Women, Patriarchy and Popular Literature* (London: Verso, 1987).

13. Alison Light, *Forever England: Femininity, Literature and Conservatism Between the Wars* (London: Routledge, 1991); Bridget Fowler, *The Alienated Reader: Women and Popular Romantic Literature in the Twentieth Century* (Brighton: Harvester Wheatsheaf, 1991).

14. Christine Gledhill, 'Pleasurable Negotiations', in E.D. Pribram (ed.), *Female Spectators: Looking at Film and Television* (London: Verso, 1988), 66.

15. Justin McCarthy, 'Novels With a Purpose', *Westminster Review*, 82 (1864), 47.

16. Geraldine Jewsbury, 'Our Library Table', *Athenaeum*, 3 December 1864, 744.

17. Ibid.

18. Jeanne Fahnestock, 'Bigamy: The Rise and Fall of a Convention', *Nineteenth Century Fiction*, 36 (1981), 65.

19. M. Oliphant, *Blackwood's*, 102 (1867), 274.

20. Elaine Showalter, 'Family Secrets and Domestic Subversion: Rebellion in the Novels of the Eighteen-Sixties', in Anthony S. Wohl (ed.), *The Victorian Family: Structure and Stresses* (London: Croom Helm, 1978), 104.

21. W. Fraser Rae, 'Sensation Novelists: Miss Braddon', *North British Review*, 43 (1865), 203.

22. Sally Shuttleworth, 'Demonic Mothers: Ideologies of Bourgeois Motherhood in the Mid-Victorian Era', in Linda Shires (ed.), *Rewriting the Victorians: Theory, History and the Politics of Gender* (London: Routledge, 1992), 32.

23. M.Oliphant, *Blackwood's*, 102 (1867), 265.

24. W. Fraser Rae, op. cit., 180.

25. See Jennifer Carnell, *The Literary Lives of M.E. Braddon* (Hastings: The Sensation Press, 2000).

26. 'Miss Braddon', *The Nation*, 9 November 1865, 593.

27. Cit., Wolff, op. cit., 126.

28. W. Fraser Rae, op. cit., 187.

29. Ibid, 186.

30. E.S. Dallas, op. cit.

31. Cit., Wolff, op. cit.,137.

32. Ann Cvetkovich, *Mixed Feelings: Feminism, Mass Culture and Victorian Sensationalism* (New Brunswick: Rutgers University Press, 1992), 50.

33. See Helena Michie, *The Flesh Made Word: Female Figures and Women's*

Bodies (Oxford: Oxford University Press, 1987).

34. For further discussion of Braddon's use of hair see Galia Ofek, 'Sensational Hair: Gender, Genre, and Fetishism in the Sensational Decade', in Kimberley Harrison and Richard Fantina (eds.), *Victorian Sensations: Essays on a Scandalous Genre* (Columbus: Ohio State University Press, 2006).

35. *Eleanor's Victory* (London: Tinsley Brothers, 1863), vol.2, 87.

36. Ibid, vol.3, 312.

37. Unsigned review of *Eleanor's Victory, Saturday Review*, 19 Sept 1863, 397.

38. W. Fraser Rae, op. cit., 191.

39. Cit., Robert Lee Wolff, 'Devoted Disciple: The Letters of Mary Elizabeth Braddon to Sir Edward Bulwer-Lytton, 1862–1873', *Harvard Library Bulletin*, 12 (1974), 25.

40. W.F. Rae, op. cit., 197. Rae did concede that *The Doctor's Wife* had 'fewer artistic faults' than Braddon's other novels, and showed 'how very nearly Miss Braddon has missed being a novelist whom we might respect and praise without reserve'.

41. Wolff, 'Devoted Disciple', 28.

42. *Birds of Prey* (London: Ward, Lock and Tyler, 1867), vol.2, 240.

43. *Charlotte's Inheritance* (London: Ward, Lock and Tyler, 1867), vol.2, 141.

44. See Jennifer Phegley, *Educating the Proper Woman Reader: Victorian Literary Family Magazines and the Cultural Health of the Nation* (Ohio: Ohio State University Press, 2004) and Solveig Robinson, 'Editing Belgravia: M.E. Braddon's Defense of Light Literature', *Victorian Periodicals Review*, 28 (1995).

45. George Augustus Sala, 'On the Sensational in Literature and Art', *Belgravia*, 4 (1868), 457–8.

46. George Augustus Sala, 'On the Cant of Modern Criticism', *Belgravia*, 4 (1867), 52.

47. *Belgravia*, 4 (1868), 41.

48. Graham Law and Andrew Maunder, *Wilkie Collins: A Literary Life* (London: Palgrave, 2008), 160.

49. 'Local Intelligence', *Sheffield and Rotherham Independent. Supplement* September 13 1884, 9.

50. 'Wyllard's Weird', *Athenaeum*, 21 March 1885, 371.

51. Ellen Wood, *Trevlyn Hold, or Squire Trevlyn's Heir* (London: Tinsley Brothers, 1864), vol.2, 132.

52. Winifred Hughes, *The Maniac in the Cellar: The Sensation Novel of the 1860s* (Princeton, NJ: Princeton University Press, 1980), 111.

53. Ibid, 155.

54. Sarah Stickney Ellis, *The Mothers of England: Their Influence and Responsibility* (London: Fisher, Son & Co., 1843), 353.

55. William Acton, *The Function and Disorders of the Reproductive Organs in Childhood, In Youth, In Adult Age, and In Advanced Life Considered In Their Physiological, Social and Psychological Relations* (London: John Churchill,1862), 102–3.
56. John Stuart Mill, *The Subjection of Women* (London: Longmans, Green, Reader and Dyer, 1869), 27.
57. Ibid.
58. Linda Williams, '"Something Else Besides a Mother": *Stella Dallas* and the Maternal Melodrama', in Christine Gledhill (ed.), *Home is Where the Heart Is: Studies in Melodrama and the Woman's Film* (London: British Film Institute, 1987), 305.
59. Hughes, op. cit., 117.
60. Ibid, 118.
61. 'Past Sensationalists', *Argosy*, December 1867, 54.
62. Cit., Jennifer Phegley, 'Domesticating the Sensation Novelist: Ellen Price Wood as Author and Editor of the *Argosy*', *Victorian Periodicals Review*, 38 (2005), 191.
63. 'Women's Novels', *The Broadway*, (1868), 504; reprinted in Maunder, *Varieties of Women's Sensation Fiction*, vol.1, 220.
64. M. Oliphant, *Blackwood's*, 102 (1867), 260.
65. 'Women's Novels', *The Broadway*, (1868), 507; reprinted in Maunder, *Varieties of Women's Sensation Fiction*, vol.1, 222.
66. Ibid.
67. See Maunder's General Introduction to the volumes in the *Varieties of Women's Sensation Fiction* series and his overview article, 'Mapping the Victorian Sensation Novel: Some Recent and Future Trends', *Literature Compass*, 2 (2005).
68. 'Women's Novels', *The Broadway*, (1868), 508; reprinted in Maunder, *Varieties of Women's Sensation Fiction*, vol.1, 223.
69. Elaine Showalter, *A Literature of Their Own: British Women Novelists from Brontë to Lessing* (Princeton: Princeton University Press, 1977), 28–9.
70. *Held in Bondage, or Granville de Vigne, a Tale of the Day* (London: Tinsley Brothers, 1863), 3 vols., vol. 1, 42. Subsequent references to this edition are given in the text.
71. *Under Two Flags* (London: Chapman and Hall, 1867), 3 vols., vol. 2, 2. Subsequent references to this edition are given in the text.
72. *Strathmore* (London: Chapman and Hall, 1865), 3 vols., vol. 1, 25. Subsequent references to this edition are given in the text.
73. *The Times*, June 6 1867, 9.
74. M. Oliphant, *Blackwood's*, 102 (1867), 268.
75. Ibid, 267.
76. The *Athenaeum*, April 20 1867, 514.
77. Tamar Heller, Introduction to *Cometh Up As A Flower*, in *Varieties of*

Women's Sensation Fiction (London: Pickering and Chatto, 2004), vol. 4, xxxv.

78. Helen Debenham offers an interesting reading of this novel in 'Rhoda Broughton's *Not Wisely But Too Well* and the Art of Sensation', in Ruth Robbins and Julian Wolfreys (eds.), *Victorian Identities: Social and Cultural Formations in Nineteenth-Century Literature,* (London: Macmillan, 1996).
79. Cit., Monica Fryckstedt, '*Geraldine Jewsbury's Athenaeum Reviews: a Mirror of Mid-Victorian Attitudes to Fiction* (Stockholm: Uppsala University Press, 1986), 87.
80. M. Oliphant, *Blackwood's*, 102 (1867), 259.
81. *Not Wisely But Too Well* (London: Cassell, 1868), 50.
82. *Spectator*, 19 October 1867, 1173.

CHAPTER 4. AFTERSHOCKS: THE SENSATION LEGACY

1. Peter Brooks, *The Melodramatic Imagination* (New Haven: Yale University Press, 1976), 22.
2. Ibid., 20.
3. Anthony Trollope, *An Autobiography*, Michael Sadleir and Michael Page (eds.), with an Introduction and Notes by P.D. Edwards (Oxford: Oxford University Press, 1923[1883]), 227.
4. Benjamin Fisher, 'A Genuine Gothic Exchange: George Meredith Pilfers Wilkie Collins's *The Dead Secret* for *Evan Harrington*', *Journal of the Georgia Philological Association*, 1 (2006), 53.
5. Sally Mitchell, *The Fallen Angel: Chastity, Class, and Women's Reading, 1835–1880* (Ohio: Bowling Green University Popular Press, 1981), 93.
6. Gordon Haight, *The George Eliot Letters*, vol. vi (New Haven and London: Yale University Press, 1956), 216.
7. H.A. Page, 'The Morality of Literary Art', *Contemporary Review*, 5 (1867), 179.
8. Barbara Hardy, Introduction to George Eliot, *Daniel Deronda* (Harmondsworth: Penguin, 1962), 27.
9. Ibid.
10. Thomas Hardy, *Desperate Remedies* (1871; London: Macmillan, 1975), 37.
11. For more on Hardy and sensation fiction see: Lawrence A. Jones, '*Desperate Remedies* and the Victorian Sensation Novel', *Nineteenth-Century Fiction*, 20(1965), 35–50; Elaine Showalter, '*Desperate Remedies*: Sensation Novels of the 1860s', *Victorian Newsletter*, 49 (1976), 1–5; Walter M. Kendrick 'The Sensationalism of Thomas Hardy', *Texas Studies in Literature and Language*, 22 (1980), 484–503.

12. Thomas Hardy, *Jude the Obscure*, ed. and intro. by Patricia Ingham (Oxford: Oxford University Press, 1985), xxxv.

13. 'Advertisements and Notices', *Belfast Newsletter*, 21 June 1883, 1.

14. Advertisement for Fanny M. Gallagher's *Thy Name is Truth: a Social Novel*, in the *Morning Post*, 17 November 1883, 7.

15. 'Local Intelligence', *Sheffield and Rotherham Independent. Supplement*, 13 September 1884, 9.

16. For a case study of the persistence of the term 'sensation' in fiction reviews, see Ellen Miller Casey, '"Highly Flavoured Dishes" and "Highly Seasoned Garbage": Sensation in the *Athenaeum*', in Kimberley Harrison and Richard Fantina (eds.), *Victorian Sensations: Essays on a Scandalous Genre* (Columbus: The Ohio State University Press, 2006), 3–14.

17. 'New Novels', *Graphic*, 21 February 1880, 202.

18. 'Some New Novels', *Standard*, 18 September 1889, 2.

19. 'Book of the Day', *Morning Post*, 6 June 1895, 6.

20. 'Books and Authors', *Hearth and Home*, 14 October 1895, 889.

21. 'Books, according to an eminent authority, are to be divided into two kinds', *Standard*, 21 February 1887, 5.

22. 'Literature', *Derby Mercury*, 16 November 1887, 6.

23. See, Nicholas Daly, 'Railway Novels: Sensation Fiction and the Modernization of the Senses', *English Literary History*, 66 (1999), 461–87 and also Chapter 2 of Daly's *Literature, Technology and Modernity, 1860–2000* (Cambridge: Cambridge University Press, 2004).

24. Lyn Pykett, 'Sensation and the Fantastic' in Deidre David (ed.), *The Cambridge Companion to The Victorian Novel* (Cambridge: Cambridge University Press, 2001), 192–211.

25. M.Oliphant, 'Sensation Novels' *Blackwood's*, 91 (May 1862), 568.

26. Anthony Trollope op. cit., 251.

27. Ronald R. Thomas, 'Detection in the Victorian Novel' in David (ed.), *The Cambridge Companion to The Victorian Novel*, 180.

28. Catherine Louisa Pirkis, *The Experiences of Loveday Brooke, Lady Detective* (London: Hutchinson, 1894), 581.

29. Ibid, 402.

30. Ibid, 402–3.

31. See Lyn Pykett, *The Improper Feminine: The Women's Sensation Novel and the New Woman Writing* (London: Routledge, 1992), 5.

32. 'Novels of the Day', *Daily News*, 6 December 1899, 7.

33. Reprinted in Norman Sherry (ed.), *Conrad: The Critical Heritage* (London: Routledge and Kegan Paul, 1973), 56.

34. Ellen Burton Harrington 'The Anarchist's Wife: Joseph Conrad's Debt to Sensation Fiction in the Secret Agent', *Conradiana: A Journal of Joseph Conrad Studies*, 36 (2004), 51.

35. Patrick Brantlinger, 'What is Sensational about the Sensation

Novel?', *Nineteenth Century* Fiction, 37(1982), 1.

36. Beth Palmer, 'Are the Victorians Still with Us?: Victorian Sensation Fiction and Its Legacies in the Twenty First Century', *Victorian Studies*, 55(2009), 87.
37. Ibid, 92.
38. Michael Faber, *The Crimson Petal and the White* (Edinburgh: Canongate, 2002), 693.
39. Ibid, 677.
40. Sarah Waters, *Affinity* (London: Virago, 1999), 91.
41. Kelly Marsh, 'The Neo-Sensation Novel: A Contemporary Genre in the Victorian Tradition', *Philological Quarterly*, 74 (1995), 111.
42. Ibid.
43. Ibid, 114.
44. 'Surrey Theatre', *The Times*, 8 November 1860, 6.
45. Zoë Aldrich, 'The Adventuress: *Lady Audley's Secret* as novel, play and film', in V. Gardner and S. Rutherford (eds.), *The New Woman and Her Sisters: Feminism and Theatre 1850–1914* (London: Methuen, 1991), 166.
46. The Literary Copyright Act of 1842 protected literary and dramatic works produced in the UK from plagiarism there, but did not prevent pirated printing of British novels outside the UK or unauthorized dramatizations of novels within the UK.
47. Patrice Pavis, *The Intercultural Performance Reader* (London: Routledge, 1996), 19.
48. See, for example, Toni Johnson-Woods, 'Mary Elizabeth Braddon in Australia: Queen of the Colonies' in Marlene Tromp, Pamela Gilbert and Aeron Hainie (eds.), *Beyond Sensation: Mary Elizabeth Braddon in Context* (Albany: SUNY Press, 2000), 111–125.
49. For further details see Katherine Mattacks, 'Regulatory Bodies: Dramatic Creativity, Control and the Commodity of *Lady Audley's Secret*', *19: Interdisciplinary Studies in the Long Nineteenth Century*, 8 (2009) www.19.bbk.ac.uk.
50. C.H. Hazelwood, *Lady Audley's Secret: An original version of Miss Braddon's popular novel in two acts*, in George Rowell (ed.), *Nineteenth Century Plays* (Oxford: Oxford University Press, 1953), Act I, scene i, 248.
51. Aldrich, op.cit.
52. Act II, scene v, 266.
53. See the Catalogue of the Lord Chamberlain's Plays, 1852–1863 on the Royal Holloway University of London website, www.rhul.ac.uk./Drama/Research/Projects/Chamberlains-plays/catalog.html
54. The Music Theatre International website http://www.mtishows.com/show_deail.asp?showid=000047
55. Andrew Maunder, '"I Will Not Live in Poverty and Neglect": *East*

Lynne on the East End Stage', in Harrison and Fantna (eds.) *Victorian Sensations*, 173–187.

56. See Martha Vicinus, '"Helpless and Unfriended": Nineteenth-Century Domestic Melodrama', *New Literary History*, 13 (1981), 127–43.

57. Maunder, op. cit., 182.

58. Letter to George Bentley, 20 February, 1875 , cit. Maunder, op. cit, 153.

59. Richard Pearson, '"Twin-Sisters" and "Theatrical Thieves": Wilkie Collins and the Dramatic Adaptation of *The Moonstone*', in Andrew Mangham (ed.), *Wilkie Collins: Interdisciplinary Essays* (Newcastle: Cambridge Scholars Press, 2007), 212.

60. See Janice Norwood, 'Sensation Drama? Collins's Stage Adaptation of *The Woman in White*' in Mangham (ed.) *Wilkie Collins: Interdisciplinary Essays*, 222–36.

61. Ibid, 229.

62. Rachel Malik, 'The Afterlife of Wilkie Collins', in Jenny Bourne Taylor (ed.), *The Cambridge Companion to Wilkie Collins* (Cambridge: Cambridge University Press, 2006), 181.

63. William Baker, Andrew Gasson, Graham Law, and Paul Lewis (eds.), *The Public Face of Wilkie Collins: The Collected Letters* (London: Pickering and Chatto, 2005), vol. 3, 177.

64. For a detailed reading of Hounam's adaptation see Jessica Cox, 'From Page to Screen: Transforming M.E. Braddon's *Lady Audley's Secret*', *Journal of Gender Studies*, 14 (2005), 23–31.

65. Ellen Wood, *East Lynne*, ed. and intro. by Elizabeth Jay (Oxford: Oxford University Press, 2005), xxxvii.

Select Bibliography

SENSATION NOVELS

In the following selection of primary texts I list an easily available modern edition (with date of first publication in volume form in square brackets), or, the first edition.

Mary Elizabeth Braddon

Lady Audley's Secret, ed. David Skilton (Oxford: Oxford University Press, 1998) [1862].

Aurora Floyd, ed. P.D. Edwards (Oxford: Oxford University Press, 1999) [1863].

Eleanor's Victory (London: Tinsley Brothers, 1863).

John Marchmont's Legacy, eds. Toru Sasaki and Norman Page (Oxford: Oxford University Press, 1999) [1863].

The Doctor's Wife, ed. Lyn Pykett (Oxford: Oxford University Press, 1998) [1864].

Henry Dunbar (London: Maxwell, 1864).

Birds of Prey (London: Ward, Lock and Tyler, 1867).

Charlotte's Inheritance (London: Ward, Lock and Tyler, 1867).

Run To Earth (London: Ward, Lock and Tyler, 1868).

Taken at the Flood (London: Maxwell, 1874).

Joshua Haggard's Daughter (London: Maxwell, 1876).

Wyllard's Weird (London: Maxwell, 1885).

Like and Unlike (London: Spencer Blackett, 1887).

Rough Justice (London: Simpkin, Marshall, Hamilton, Ken & Co, 1898).

Rhoda Broughton

Cometh Up As A Flower, ed. Pamela Gilbert (Peterborough, Ontario: Broadview Press, 2010) [1867].

155

Not Wisely But Too Well (London: Cassell, 1867).

Wilkie Collins

The Woman in White, ed. John Sutherland (Oxford: Oxford University Press, 1996) [1860].

No Name, ed. Virginia Blain (Oxford: Oxford University Press, 1998) [1862].

Armadale, ed. Catherine Peters (Oxford: Oxford University Press, 1999) [1866].

The Moonstone, ed. John Sutherland (Oxford: Oxford University Press, 1999) [1868].

Man and Wife, ed. Norman Page (Oxford: Oxford University Press, 1995) [1870].

The New Magdalen (London: Richard Bentley, 1873).

The Law and the Lady, ed. Jenny Bourne Taylor (Oxford: Oxford University Press, 1999) [1875].

Jezebel's Daughter (London: Chatto and Windus, 1880).

Heart and Science, ed. Steve Farmer (Peterborough, Ontario: Broadview Press, 1996) [1883].

Annie Edward[e]s

The Morals of Mayfair (London: Hurst and Blackett, 1858).

The World's Verdict (London: Hurst and Blackett, 1860).

The Ordeal for Wives (London: Hurst and Blackett, 1864).

Ought We to Visit Her? (London: Bentley, 1871).

A Vagabond Heroine (London: Bentley, 1873).

Leah, a Woman of Fashion (London: Bentley, 1875).

Florence Marryat

Love's Conflict ed. Andrew Maunder, *Varieties of Women's Sensation Fiction, 1855–1890* (London: Pickering and Chatto, 2004), vol.2. [1865].

Too Good for Him (London: Bentley, 1865).

Woman Against Woman (London: Bentley, 1865).

The Confessions of Gerald Estcourt (London: Bentley, 1867).

Nelly Brooke (London: Bentley, 1868).

Veronique (London: Bentley, 1869).

The Girls of Feversham (London: Bentley, 1869).

Annie Thomas

Played Out (London: Chapman and Hall, 1866).

Called to Account (London: Tinsley Brothers, 1867).

156

Ouida

Held in Bondage, or Granville de Vigne, a Tale of the Day (London: Tinsley Brothers, 1863).
Strathmore (London: Chapman and Hall, 1865).
Under Two Flags (London: Chapman and Hall, 1867).

Ellen Wood

East Lynne, ed. Elisabeth Jay (Oxford: Oxford University Press, 2004) [1861].
Verner's Pride (London: Richard Bentley, 1863).
Lord Oakburn's Daughters (London: Richard Bentley, 1864).
Trevlyn Hold (London: Richard Bentley, 1864).
St Martin's Eve, ed. Lyn Pykett, *Varieties of Women's Sensation Fiction, 1855–1890* (London: Pickering and Chatto, 2004), vol. 3 [1866].
Roland Yorke (London: Bentley, 1869).
Bessy Rane (London: Bentley, 1870).
George Canterbury's Will (London: Tinsley Brothers, 1870).
Within the Maze (London: Bentley, 1872).
The Story of Charles Strange (London: Bentley, 1888).

NINETEENTH-CENTURY REVIEWS AND ARTICLES ON SENSATION FICTION

Anon, 'Esmond and Basil', *Bentley's Miscellany* 32 (1852), 576–86.
———, 'Our Female Sensation Novelists', *Christian Remembrancer*, 46 (1863), 209–36.
———, 'Sensation', *The Literary Times*, 9 May 1863, 102–3.
———, 'Sensational Novels', *Medical Critic and Psychological Journal*, 3 (1863), 513–9.
———, 'The Queen's English', *Edinburgh Review*, 120 (1864), 37–57.
———, 'The Sensational Williams', *All the Year Round*, 13 February 1864, 14–17.
———, 'Sensational Literature', *The Christian Observer*, 335 (1865), 809–13.
———, 'Belles Lettres', *Westminster Review*, 2 (1866), 269–70.
———, 'Madness in Novels', *Spectator*, 3 February 1866, 135–6.
———, 'Women's Novels', *The Broadway*, n.s. 1 (1868), 504–9.
———, 'Past "Sensationalists"', *Argosy*, December 1867, 59–56.
Austin, Alfred, 'Our Novels: The Sensational School', *Temple Bar*, 29 (1870), 137–43.

Chorley, H.F., 'Armadale', *Athenaeum*, 2 June 1866, 732–3.

Dallas, E.S., 'Lady Audley's Secret', *The Times*, 18 November 1862, 8.

James, Henry, 'Miss Braddon', *The Nation*, 9 November 1865, 593–5. Reprinted in *Notes and Reviews* (Cambridge, Mass: Harvard University Press, 1981, 108–16).

Jewsbury, Geraldine, 'Our Library Table', *Athenaeum*, 3 December 1864, 744.

————, 'Cometh Up as a Flower', *Athenaeum*, 20 April 1867, 514–5.

McCarthy, J., 'Novels with a purpose', *Westminster Review*, 82 (1864), 24–49.

Mansel, H.L., (1863) 'Sensation Novels', *Quarterly Review*, 133 (1863), 481–514.

Oliphant, M., 'Sensation Novels', *Blackwood's*, 91 (1862), 464–84.

————, 'Novels', *Blackwood's*, 94 (1863), 168–83.

————, 'Novels', *Blackwood's*, 102 (1867), 257–80.

Paget, Frances, Afterword to *Lucretia: or the Heroine of the Nineteenth Century* (London: J. Masters, 1868).

Rae, W. F. 'Sensation novelists: Miss Braddon', *North British Review*, 43 (1865), 180–204.

Sala, George, Augustus, 'The Cant of Modern Criticism', *Belgravia*, 4 (1867), 45–55.

————, 'On The "Sensational" in Literature and Art' *Belgravia*, 4 (1868), 449-58.

THE SENSATION NOVEL AND SENSATION NOVELISTS (TWENTIETH-CENTURY STUDIES)

Aldrich, Zoë, 'The Adventuress: *Lady Audley's Secret* as novel, play and film', in V. Gardner and S. Rutherford (eds.), *The New Woman and Her Sisters: Feminism and Theatre 1850–1914* (London: Methuen, 1991), 159–74.

Bachman, Maria K., and Don Richard Cox (eds.) *Reality's Dark Light: The Sensational Wilkie Collins* (Knoxville: University of Tennessee Press, 2003).

Bernstein, Susan, 'Dirty Reading: Sensation Fiction, Women and Primitivism', *Criticism*, 36 (1994), 213–41.

Boyle, Thomas, *Black Swine in the Sewers of Hampstead: Beneath the Surface of Victorian Sensationalism* (London: Hodder and Stoughton, 1989).

Brantlinger, Patrick, 'What is Sensational About the Sensation Novel?', *Nineteenth Century Fiction*, 37 (1982), 1–28.

Carnell, Jennifer, *The Literary Lives of M.E. Braddon* (Hastings: The Sensation Press, 2000).

Casey, Ellen Miller, '"Other People's Prudery": Mary Elizabeth Braddon', in Don Richard Cox (ed.), *Sexuality and Victorian Literature* (Knoxville: University of Tennessee Press, 1984), 72–82.

Cox, Jessica, 'From Page to Screen: Transforming M.E. Braddon's *Lady Audley's Secret*', *Journal of Gender Studies*, 14 (2005), 23–31.

Cvetkovich, Ann, 'Ghostlier Determinations: the Economy of Sensation and *The Woman in White*', *Novel*, 23 (1989), 24–43.

———, *Mixed Feelings: Feminism, Mass Culture and Victorian Sensationalism* (New Brunswick: Rutgers University Press, 1992).

Daly, Nicholas, 'Railway Novels: Sensation Fiction and the Modernization of the Senses', *English Literary History*, 66 (1999), 461–87.

———, *Literature, Technology and Modernity, 1860–2000* (Cambridge: Cambridge University Press, 2004).

Debenham, Helen, 'Rhoda Broughton's *Not Wisely But Too Well* and the Art of Sensation', in Ruth Robbins and Julian Wolfreys (eds.), *Victorian Identities: Social and Cultural Formations in Nineteenth-Century Literature* (London: Macmillan, 1996), 9–24.

Eliot, T. S., 'Wilkie Collins and Dickens', *Times Literary Supplement*, 4 August 1927, 525–26; reprinted in *Selected Essays: 1917–1932* (London: Faber, 1932).

Edwards, P.D., *Some Mid-Victorian Thrillers: The Sensation Novel, Its Friends and Its Foes* (St. Lucia: Queensland University Press, 1971).

Fahnestock, Jeanne, 'Bigamy: the Rise and Fall of a Convention', *Nineteenth Century Fiction*, 36 (1981), 47–71.

Gruner, Elizabeth Rose, 'Plotting the Mother: Caroline Norton, Helen Huntington, and Isabel Vane,' *Tulsa Studies in Women's Literature*, 16 (1997), 303–25.

Harrison, Kimberley and Richard Fantina (eds.), *Victorian Sensations: Essays on a Scandalous Genre* (Columbus: Ohio State University Press, 2006).

Heller, Tamar, *Dead Secrets: Wilkie Collins and the Female Gothic* (New Haven: Yale University Press, 1992).

———, 'Recent Work on Victorian Gothic and Sensation Fiction', *Victorian Literature and Culture*, 24 (1996), 349–66.

Hughes, Winifred, *The Maniac in the Cellar: the Sensation Novel of the 1860s* (Princeton, NJ: Princeton University Press, 1980).

Jones, Lawrence A., '*Desperate Remedies* and the Victorian Sensation Novel', *Nineteenth-Century Fiction*, 20 (1965), 35–50.

Kaplan, Elizabeth, A., 'The Political Unconscious in the Maternal Melodrama: Ellen Wood's *East Lynne* (1861)', in Derek Longhurst, *Gender, Genre and Narrative Pleasure* (London: Methuen, 1989).

Kendrick, Walter, M. 'The Sensationalism of *The Woman in White*', *Nineteenth Century Fiction*, 32 (1977), 18–35.

———, 'The Sensationalism of Thomas Hardy', *Texas Studies in*

Literature and Language, 22 (1980), 484–503.

Kent, Christopher, 'Probability, Reality and Sensation in the Novels of Wilkie Collins', *Dickens Studies Annual*, 20 (1991), 259–80.

King, Andrew, 'Sympathy as Subversion? Reading *Lady Audley's Secret* in the Kitchen', *Journal of Victorian Culture*, 7 (2002), 60–85.

Knoepflmacher, Ulrich, C., 'The Counterworld of Victorian Fiction and *The Woman in White*' in Jerome H. Buckley (ed.), *The Worlds of Victorian Fiction* (Cambridge, Mass.: Harvard University Press, 1975).

Law, Graham and Andrew Maunder, *Wilkie Collins: A Literary Life* (Basingstoke: Palgrave, 2008).

Liddle, Dallas, 'Anatomy of a "Nine Day's Wonder": Sensational Journalism in the Decade of the Sensation Novel', in Andrew Maunder and Grace Moore (eds.), *Victorian Crime, Madness and Sensation* (Aldershot: Ashgate, 2004).

Liggins, Emma, 'Good Housekeeping? Domestic Economy and Suffering Wives in Mrs Henry Wood's Early Fiction', in Emma Liggins and Daniel Duffy (eds.) *Feminist Readings of Victorian Popular Texts: Divergent Femininities* (Aldershot: Ashgate, 2001).

Loesberg, Jonathan, 'The Ideology of Narrative Form in Sensation Fiction', *Representations*, 13 (1986), 115–38.

Mangham, Andrew (ed.), *Wilkie Collins: Interdisciplinary Essays* (Newcastle: Cambridge Scholars Press, 2007).

Marsh, Kelly, 'The Neo-Sensation Novel: A Contemporary Genre in the Victorian Tradition', *Philological Quarterly*, 74 (1995), 99–123.

Mattacks, Katherine, 'Regulatory Bodies: Dramatic Creativity, Control and the Commodity of *Lady Audley's Secret*', 19: *Interdisciplinary Studies in the Long Nineteenth Century*, 8 (2009) www.19.bbk.ac.uk.

Maunder, Andrew 'Mapping the Victorian Sensation Novel', *Literature Compass*, 2 (2005).

Maunder, Andrew and Grace Moore (eds.), *Victorian Crime, Madness and Sensation* (Aldershot: Ashgate, 2004).

Miller, D.A., '*Cage aux Folles*: Sensation Fiction and Gender in Wilkie Collins's *the Woman in White*', *Representations*, 14 (1986), 107–36.

Nayder, Lillian, *Wilkie Collins*, (New York: Twayne, 1997).

Ofek, Galia, 'Sensational Hair: Gender, Genre, and Fetishism in the Sensational Decade', in Kimberley Harrison and Richard Fantina, (eds.), *Victorian Sensations: Essays on a Scandalous Genre* (Columbus: Ohio State University Press, 2006).

Page, Norman, *Wilkie Collins, The Critical Heritage* (London: Routledge and Kegan Paul, 1974).

Palmer, Beth, 'Are the Victorians Still with Us?: Victorian Sensation Fiction and Its Legacies in the Twenty First Century', *Victorian Studies*, 55 (2009), 86–94.

Phegley, Jennifer, '"Henceforward I Refuse to Bow the Knee to Their

Narrow Rule": Mary Elizabeth Braddon's *Belgravia* Magazine, Women Readers, and Literary Valuation', *Nineteenth-Century Contexts*, 26 (2004), 149–71.

———, 'Domesticating the Sensation Novelist: Ellen Price Wood as Author and Editor of the *Argosy*', *Victorian Periodicals Review*, 38 (2005), 180–98.

———, 'Teaching Genre: The Sensation Novel' in Andrew Maunder and Jennifer Phegley (eds.), *Teaching Nineteenth-Century Fiction* (Basingstoke: Palgrave, 2010), 91–108.

Pykett, Lyn, *The Improper Feminine: The Women's Sensation Novel and the New Woman Writing* (London: Routledge, 1992).

———, *Wilkie Collins, Contemporary Critical Essays* (Basingstoke: Macmillan, 1998).

———, 'Sensation and the Fantastic', in Deidre David (ed.), *The Cambridge Companion to The Victorian Novel* (Cambridge: Cambridge University Press, 2001).

———, 'The Newgate Novel and Sensation Fiction, 1830–1868', in Martin Priestman (ed.), *The Cambridge Companion to Crime Fiction* (Cambridge: Cambridge University Press, 2003).

———, *Wilkie Collins* (Oxford: Oxford University Press, 2005).

Radford, Andrew, *Victorian Sensation Fiction: A Reader's Guide to Essential Criticism* (Basingstoke: Palgrave Macmillan, 2009).

Robbins, Ruth and Julian Wolfreys (eds.), *Victorian Gothic: Literary and Cultural Manifestations in the Nineteenth Century* (Basingstoke: Palgrave Macmillan, 2002).

Robinson, Solveig, 'Editing Belgravia: M.E. Braddon's Defense of Light Literature', *Victorian Periodicals Review*, 28 (1995), 109–22.

Schroeder, Natalie, 'Feminine Sensationalism, Eroticism, and Self-Assertion: M.E. Braddon and Ouida', *Tulsa Studies in Women's Literature*, 7 (1988), 87–103.

Showalter, Elaine, *A Literature of Their Own: British Women Novelists from Brontë to Lessing* (Princeton: Princeton University Press, 1977).

———, 'Family Secrets and Domestic Subversion: Rebellion in the Novels of the Eighteen-Sixties', in Anthony S. Wohl (ed.), *The Victorian Family: Structure and Stresses* (London: Croom Helm, 1978).

———, '*Desperate Remedies*: Sensation Novels of the 1860s', *Victorian Newsletter*, 49 (1976), 1–5.

Taylor, Jenny Bourne, *In the Secret Theatre of Home: Wilkie Collins, Sensation Narrative and Nineteenth-Century Psychology* (London: Routledge, 1988).

———, (ed.), *The Cambridge Companion to Wilkie Collins* (Cambridge: Cambridge University Press, 2006).

Tromp, Marlene, Pamela Gilbert and Aeron Hainie (eds.), *Beyond Sensation: Mary Elizabeth Braddon in Context* (Albany: SUNY Press,

2000).

Wolff, Robert, Lee, *Sensational Victorian: The Life and Fiction of Mary Elizabeth Braddon* (New York: Garland, 1997).

———, 'Devoted Disciple: The Letters of Mary Elizabeth Braddon to Sir Edward Bulwer-Lytton, 1862–1873', *Harvard Library Bulletin*, 12 (1974), 1–35 and 129–61.

Wynne, Deborah, *The Sensation Novel and the Victorian Family Magazine* (Basingstoke: Palgrave, 2001).

THE LITERARY AND SOCIAL CONTEXT OF THE SENSATION NOVEL

Acton, William, *The Functions and Disorders of the Reproductive Organs in Childhood, In Youth, In Adult Age, and In Advanced Life Considered in their Physiological, Social and Psychological Relations* (London: John Churchill, 1862).

Anderson, Amanda, *Tainted Souls and Painted Faces: The Rhetoric of Fallenness in Victorian Culture* (Ithaca: Cornell University Press, 1993).

Armstrong, Nancy, *Desire and Domestic Fiction* (New York: Oxford University Press, 1987).

Austin, Alfred, 'The Poetry of the Period: Mr Swinburne', *Temple Bar*, 26 (1869), 457–74.

William Baker, Andrew Gasson, Graham Law, and Paul Lewis (eds.), *The Public Face of Wilkie Collins: The Collected Letters* (London: Pickering and Chatto, 2005), 4 vols.

Booth, Michael, *Victorian Spectacular Theatre, 1850–1910* (London: Routledge, 1981).

Brantlinger, Patrick, *The Reading Lesson: The Threat of Mass Literacy in the Nineteenth Century* (Bloomington: Indiana University Press, 1998).

Brooks, Peter, *The Melodramatic Imagination* (New Haven: Yale University Press, 1976).

———, *Reading for the Plot: Design and Intention in Narrative* (New York: Knopf, 1984).

Clarke, William, *The Secret Life of Wilkie Collins* (London: Allison & Busby, 1988)

Collins, Wilkie, *My Miscellanies* (London: Sampson Low, 1863).

Ellis, Sarah Stickney, *The Mothers of England, Their Influence and Responsibility* (London: Fisher, Son & Co., 1843).

Flint, Kate, *The Woman Reader, 1837–1914* (Oxford: Oxford University Press, 1993).

Fowler, Bridget, *The Alienated Reader: Women and Popular Romantic*

Literature in the Twentieth Century (Brighton: Harvester Wheatsheaf, 1991).

Gilbert, Pamela, *Disease, Desire and the Body in Victorian Women's Popular Novels* (Cambridge: Cambridge University Press, 2005).

Gill, Rebecca, 'The Imperial Anxieties of a Nineteenth-Century Bigamy Case', *History Workshop Journal* 57 (2004), 58–78.

Hadley, Elaine, *Melodramatic Tactics: Theatricalized Dissent in the English Marketplace, 1800–1885* (Stanford: Stanford University Press, 1995).

Helsinger, Elizabeth.K. et al (eds.), *The Woman Question: Society and Literature in Britain and America, 1837–1883* (Manchester: Manchester University Press, 1983), 3 vols. Volume three is particularly useful for the study of the sensation novel.

Holcombe, Lee, 'Victorian Wives and Property: Reform of the Married Woman's Property Law, 1857–1882', in Martha Vicinus (ed.), *A Widening Sphere: Changing Roles of Victorian Women* (London: Routledge, 1980), 3–28.

Hughes, Linda and Michael Lund, *The Victorian Serial* (Charlottesville: University of Virginia Press, 1991).

Kalikoff, Beth, *Murder and Moral Decay in Victorian Popular Literature* (Ann Arbor, Michigan: University of Michigan Press, 1986).

Law, Graham, *Serializing Fiction in the Victorian Press* (Basingstoke: Macmillan, 2000).

Linton, E. L., 'The Girl of the Period', *Saturday Review*, 14 March 1868, 339–40.

Meisel, Martin, *Realizations: Narrative, Pictorial and Theatrical Arts in Nineteenth-Century England* (Princeton: Princeton University Press, 1983).

Michie, Helena, *The Flesh Made Word: Female Figures and Women's Bodies* (Oxford: Oxford University Press, 1987).

Mill, John Stuart, *The Subjection of Women* (London: Longmans, Green, Reader and Dyer, 1869).

Mitchell, Sally, 'Sentiment and Suffering: Women's Recreational Reading in the 1860s', *Victorian Studies*, 21 (1977), 29–45.

———, *The Fallen Angel: Chastity, Class, and Women's Reading, 1835–1880* (Ohio: Bowling Green University Popular Press, 1981).

Phegley, Jennifer, *Educating the Proper Woman Reader: Victorian Literary Family Magazines and the Cultural Health of the Nation* (Ohio: Ohio State University Press, 2004).

Poovey, Mary, *Uneven Developments: The Ideological Work of Gender in Mid-Victorian England* (Chicago: University of Chicago Press, 1988).

Richards, Thomas, *The Commodity Culture of Victorian England: Advertising and Spectacle, 1851–1914* (Stanford: Stanford University Press, 1990).

Rowell, George (ed.), *Nineteenth Century Plays* (Oxford: Oxford

University Press, 1953).

Rubery, Matthew, *The Novelty of Newspapers: Victorian Fiction After the Invention of the News* (Oxford: Oxford University Press, 2009).

Showalter, Elaine, *The Female Malady: Women, Madness and Culture, 1830–1980* (London: Virago, 1987).

Shuttleworth, Sally, 'Demonic Mothers: Ideologies of Bourgeois Motherhood in the Mid-Victorian Era', in Linda Shires (ed.), *Rewriting the Victorians: Theory, History and the Politics of Gender* (London: Routledge, 1992), 31–51.

Small, Helen, *Love's Madness: Medicine, the Novel and Female Insanity, 1800–1865* (Oxford: Oxford University Press, 1996).

Thompson, Nicola Diane, *Reviewing Sex: Gender and the Reception of Victorian Novels* (New York: New York University Press, 1996).

Tillotson, Kathleen, 'The Lighter Reading of the Eighteen-Sixties', Introduction to Wilkie Collins, *The Woman in White* (Boston: Houghton Mifflin, 1969).

Tompkins, Jane, *Sensational Designs: The Cultural Work of American Fiction, 1790–1860* (Oxford: Oxford University Press, 1985).

Trodd, Anthea, *Domestic Crime and the Victorian Novel* (Basingstoke: Macmillan, 1989).

Vicinus, Martha, *Suffer and Be Still: Women in the Victorian Age* (London: Methuen,1980 [1972]).

———, *A Widening Sphere: Changing Roles of Victorian Women* (London: Methuen, 1980 [1977]).

———, '"Helpless and Unfriended": Nineteenth-Century Domestic Melodrama', *New Literary History*, 13 (1981), 127–43.

Williams, Raymond, *The English Novel From Dickens to Lawrence* (London: Hogarth Press, 1985).

Winter, Alison, *Mesmerized: Powers of Mind in Victorian Britain* (Chicago: Chicago University Press, 1998).

STUDIES OF POPULAR CULTURE

Fowler, Bridget, *The Alienated Reader: Women and Popular Romantic Literature in the Twentieth Century* (Brighton: Harvester Wheatsheaf, 1991).

Gledhill, Christine (ed.), *Home is Where the Heart is: Studies in Melodrama and the Woman's Film* (London: British Film Institute, 1987).

———, 'Pleasurable Negotiations', in E.D. Pribram (ed.), *Female Spectators: Looking at Film and Television* (London: Verso, 1988).

Light, Alison, *Forever England: Femininity, Literature and Conservatism Between The Wars* (London: Routledge, 1991).

Modleski, Tania, *Loving With a Vengeance: Mass-Produced Fantasies for*

Women (London: Methuen, 1984).

Pavis, Patrice (ed.), *The Intercultural Performance Reader* (London: Routledge, 1996).

Radway, Janice, *Reading the Romance: Women, Patriarchy and Popular Literature* (London: Verso, 1987).

Williams, Linda, '"Something Else Besides a Mother": *Stella Dallas* and the Maternal Melodrama', in Christine Gledhill (ed.), *Home is Where the Heart Is: Studies in Melodrama and the Woman's Film* (London: British Film Institute, 1987).

Index